ON THE GO WITH SENIOR SERVICES

ON THE GO WITH SENIOR SERVICES

LIBRARY PROGRAMS FOR ANY TIME AND ANY PLACE

Phyllis Goodman

LIBRARIES
UNLIMITED®
An Imprint of ABC-CLIO, LLC
Santa Barbara, California • Denver, Colorado

Copyright © 2020 by Phyllis Goodman

Library of Congress Cataloging in Publication Control Number: 2019917197

ISBN: 978-1-4408-7228-0 (paperback)
      978-1-4408-7229-7 (ebook)

24 23 22 21 20   1 2 3 4 5

This book is also available as an eBook.

Libraries Unlimited
An Imprint of ABC-CLIO, LLC

ABC-CLIO, LLC
147 Castilian Drive
Santa Barbara, California 93117
www.abc-clio.com

This book is printed on acid-free paper ∞

Manufactured in the United States of America

For Charlotte and Priscilla

CONTENTS

PREFACE

Research shows that the older adult population is growing and will continue to grow for the next several decades. They are a diverse group with a variety of needs and backgrounds. While some older adults are mobile, there are those who, for cognitive and physical reasons, are living with family, in residential and assisted living facilities, or spend part of their day in adult day care. The adult population has different needs at different points in their life though programming for older adults is often lumped together with all adult library programming. There have been books published about creating adult services and programming in the library; however, programming for older adults who are not able to visit the library is often briefly, if at all, talked about in the literature.

The idea for *On the Go with Senior Services: Library Programs for Any Time and Any Place* began before I retired from my full-time position as adult services librarian. Like so many other adult services librarians, in the public library, senior outreach was only one part of my responsibilities and one that I did not have a lot of training for. Unfortunately, I found few resources about programming for older adults, especially ones that would help me create programs that used library materials, were fun and educational, and included opportunities to reminisce and interact with others.

My outreach programs took me to facilities where residents lived with a variety of physical and cognitive illnesses. Some residents were mobile; some were in wheelchairs. Others were heavily medicated and unable to communicate. What was interesting was that most of the residents were very interested in attending the programs and enjoyed interacting and learning with others. Even those who were not communicative seemed to be listening and enjoying the stories. To meet the needs of these different groups, I used some of the techniques and skills I had used for story times during my early career as a youth services librarian. The format I used started with a theme and included a lot of different materials that went along with that theme—activities, books, games, photos and pictures, slide shows, and crafts. With the information I gathered, I was able to use the same program and adapt it to the needs of the group I was working with.

This book contains research and information about who the older adult population is and how the perception of aging is changing. Research shows that older adults do continue to learn and benefit from interacting with others and engaging in activities that stimulate thinking. When doing research for this book, I reached out to other libraries around the country and found that there are many libraries that still offer traditional homebound and book collection services. However, many are beginning to expand those services to story time programs, memory cafés, off-site computer classes, storytelling, and art-based programs. The problem is that these types of programs and informative information about older adults are, often, not reflected in the literature.

This book is a place for librarians to start becoming more familiar with whom the older adult population is and the possibilities for programming, but it is by no means comprehensive. It contains a variety of programs for older adults obtained from libraries around the country. All can be used in the library; taken off-site to assisted living facilities, nursing homes, adult day care, and memory cafés; or made into kits to be checked out from the library. The format of these programs can also be used as is or as a springboard for creating other programs. It is my hope that library staff will share their programs and experiences with others and will explore ways to expand their services for this population. Programming for the older adult just makes sense as it meets a library's goal of lifelong learning.

ACKNOWLEDGMENTS

This book would not have been a reality if it were not for the support and input from peers, friends, and family. I appreciate and am grateful for all their support. To the editors and staff at Libraries Unlimited, thank you for helping me put together a well-rounded proposal that resulted in this book being accepted for publication. Many thanks to Jessica Gribble, for answering my many questions, taking me on after a staffing change, and helping to bring this book to completion.

This book would not have been complete without the input of library staff from around the country who were very willing to share their programs and ideas for older adults. First, I would like to thank two of my contributors Mary Beth Riedner and Adam Chang who provided firsthand experience and information about memory loss and technology literacy. These issues affect the lives of many in the older adult population, and libraries are in a position to address these concerns. Special thanks to Mary Beth Riedner, retired librarian and creator of the Tales and Travels Memories program, for her information about dementia and how library staff can work and program for persons diagnosed with this disease and their caregivers. Special thanks to Adam Chang, instruction and research librarian, Central Ridge Library, Florida, for providing information about providing technology classes when a dedicated computer lab is not available.

I am very thankful and honored that so many libraries and staff were willing to provide program outlines to include in the book. My thanks to Jennifer Baugh, Six Mile Regional Library District, Illinois; Jennifer Bishop, Carroll County Public Library, Maryland; Barbara Brown, Peoria Public Library, Illinois; Marie Corbitt, Westerville Public Library, Ohio; Carlye Dennis, Fayetteville Public Library, Arkansas; Mary Fahndrich, Madison Public Library, Wisconsin; Julie Hyland, Music & Memory program, Wisconsin; Jackson District Public Library, Michigan; Mary Kay Johnson, Norwalk Easter Public Library, Iowa; Valerie Lewis, Suffolk Cooperative Library System, New York; Alyson Low, Fayetteville Public Library, Arkansas; Stacey McKim, Iowa City Public Library, Iowa; Loanis Menendez, Delray Beach Public Library, Florida; Tiffany Meyer, Ellsworth Public Library, Wisconsin; Angela Meyers, Bridges Library System, Wisconsin; Missoula Public Library, Montana; Cari Pierce, Peoria Public Library, Illinois; Dorothy Stoltz, Carroll County Public Library, Maryland; Alyson Walzer, Delray Beach Public Library, Florida; and Judith Wright, Homewood Public Library, Alabama.

Many special thanks to my husband Jeff for his support and encouragement and making sure we had dinner on the table during the months I was writing. To my son, Steven, who inspires me to step outside of my comfort zone. I love you much.

INTRODUCTION

The concept of learning and education is often synonymous with libraries. Libraries have been educational centers almost since their inception. Andrew Carnegie considered public libraries educational centers for everyone when his foundation funded the construction of over 2,500 public libraries in the late nineteenth and early twentieth centuries. The public library was the center of education for new immigrants coming to the United States, in the early twentieth century, wanting to obtain citizenship information. It is a place to learn about current events and, more recently, a center for lifelong learning that has been embraced by public libraries as an important part of their mission statement. Libraries promote lifelong learning by offering computer classes and a computer lab, services and programs that promote reading through book clubs and current affairs groups. They promote cultural literacy through speakers, music, festivals, and other cultural events and are a meeting place for test preparation and English-as-a-second-language classes (Elmborg, 2016; Gilton, 2016).

"Lifelong learning" is a term used to describe formal and nonformal learning from birth to grave. Public libraries have generally divided their population into three age groups—childhood (birth to twelve years), young adult (thirteen to seventeen years), and adults (eighteen years and older). Lifelong learning for the younger population often refers to learning that takes place in an educational institution. Lifelong learning for the adult population refers to learning obtained after one completes a formal education program and can be found in a variety of settings, including libraries, museums, and senior centers. Library programming and services for the adult population often includes the entire adult population, which covers a wide spectrum of ages and life events (Okobi, 2014; Von Doetinchem, 2019).

The adult population is a large and diverse population, and their needs change as they age. At the younger end of the spectrum, adults are beginning careers and establishing families. In the middle years, they are raising children, switching careers, and sending their children off to college and jobs. They may be caring for an elderly family member and trying to save for retirement. At the other end of the spectrum, adults sixty years and older are planning for retirement; they may be dealing with health issues, which restrict their mobility or need to plan for long-term care. Within every community there will also be cultural, economic, and racial factors that impact the needs and experiences of the adult population. The one-size-fits-all approach may have been enough at one time, but in the twenty-first century libraries need to understand the needs of the entire adult population and plan programs and services that meet these needs.

The baby boomer generation, those born between 1946 and 1964, started turning sixty-five in 2011 and have had a major impact on older adult services and programming. This generation is healthier and better educated, supports libraries, and wants to continue learning. Due to technological and health advances more people are living longer, into their eighties and nineties. Some are mobile, and some are living in senior facilities, or with family members. They attend adult day care and memory cafés or may have early-stage dementia or Alzheimer's disease.

Schull (2013) discusses in her book *50+ Services* about the lack of programming for the older adult population who are not able to visit the library. This population is growing though they are often included in the overall discussion of adult programming, not as a separate group with specific needs. The Adult Services division of the American Library Association (ALA) in 2017 updated its guidelines on services and programming for older adults. It increased the age of the older adult demographic from fifty-five years to sixty years and older; it placed more emphasis on adult programs that created lifelong learning with emphasis on computer training and working with other agencies in the community that work with the older population. Providing services to the homebound and those living in senior facilities such as assisted living, nursing homes, senior centers, residential care communities, and senior day care was an important addition. There are libraries that are changing their policies on older adult services; however, there are still problems with how older adults are perceived and how programming is divided (Okobi, 2014; Reference and User Services Association, 2017; Schull, 2013).

Many excellent books have been written in the past few years on creating and implementing adult services in the public library. These books discuss and provide examples of how to do an assessment of the community, gaining support and programming for older adults (fifty-five plus) who visit the library. Often missing in these books is an in-depth look at programming for adults who are not able to visit the library. In some cases there might be a paragraph or perhaps a chapter about the importance of outreach and a brief description of some programs. The programs most often cited are journaling programs, homebound services, and book collection drop-offs. In addition to the perception of older adults being dependent, unable and unwilling to learn and try new things, Schull (2013) points to other factors that keep libraries from making changes in services for the older adult population. She states that staff size and budget, with some libraries having only one or maybe two adult service librarians, may strain their ability to try new services. Lack of a forum to share ideas and resources between librarians who may be looking for new ways to program and lack of formal training for working with older adult populations contribute to the lack of more library services that meet the needs of the growing older adult population. I found this still to be true (Schull, 2013).

SCOPE

This book, *On the Go with Senior Services: Library Programs for Any Time and Any Place*, is a resource for adult services library staff who are looking for programs to use with the older adult population or want to expand what they are doing now. The focus of this book is on the older adult, aged sixty years and older, who is not able to visit the library. There are outlines of programs and services from around the country that may be used at a variety of locations—senior communities, assisted living, early dementia and Alzheimer's centers, nursing homes, rehab centers, adult day care, memory cafés, and the library. They may be used as is or as a springboard to creating programs to fit a library's needs. A discussion about the characteristics of the older adult population and misinformation about aging is included. Creating programs for this population, doing a library and community assessment, using volunteers, and working with local community organizations are also discussed.

ORGANIZATION

On the Go with Senior Services: Library Programs for Any Time and Any Place began as an idea to share programs and information about working with the older adult population with library staff who work with older adults. It soon became clear that for this book to be well rounded it needed to include a variety of programs that had been used successfully with older adults who were not able to visit the library. Research for the book began with a post on Programming Librarian on Facebook asking librarians if they offered programs for older adults who were not able to visit the library. Those who responded were contacted about their programs and asked if they would give permission to include a description and outline of their program and any suggestions/tips they could offer other librarians who worked with older adults. Those who responded and gave permission are included in the programs section. I also browsed library websites using the LibWeb list of library servers on the WWW (LibWeb, 2018). Most of the library websites that were browsed offered homebound and book delivery services. However, I did find some interesting programs that were being offered, and I contacted those libraries as well.

Part I of this book includes a discussion about the characteristics and experiences of the older adult population as well as the physical and cognitive issues they face. Planning and evaluating library services for this population is discussed, and programming ideas and suggestion/tips for working with this population are included.

Part II of this book, "The Programs," includes program outlines from libraries around the country that meet different needs of the older adult population in their community. There are programs for caregivers and patrons with dementia, art-based programs, and computer programs. All the programs include a description and outline of the program, ways to expand on the ideas, and suggestions/tips for working with older adults. They can be used in a variety of ways—as an outreach kit, as a workshop training tool, or made into kits that can be checked out. They are the beginning of networking with other librarians who want to expand programs and services for the older nonmobile adult population.

REFERENCES

Elmborg, James. April 2016 (Winter). "Tending the Garden of Learning: Lifelong Learning as Core Library Value." *Library Trends* 64 (no. 3). 533–555. https://ir.uiowa.edu/cgi/viewcontent.cgi?article=1021&context=slis_pubs.

Gilton, Donna. 2016. *Creating and Promoting Lifelong Learning in Public Libraries.* Lanham, MD: Rowman & Littlefield.

LibWeb. 2018. lib-web.org/united-states/public-libraries.

Okobi, Elsie A. Rogers Halliday. 2014. *Library Services for Adults in the 21st Century.* Santa Barbara, CA: Libraries Unlimited.

Reference and User Services Association. September 2017. "Guidelines for Library Services with 60+ Audiences: Best Practices." American Library Association, Chicago. http://www.ala.org/rusa/sites/ala.org.rusa/files/content/resources/guidelines/60plusGuidelines2017.pdf.

Schull, Diantha Dow. 2013. *50+ Library Services.* Chicago: American Library Association. ALA Editions.

Von Doetinchem, Sandra. January 19, 2019. "Lifelong Learning: Do You Know It When You See It?" American Society on Aging. https://www.asaging.org/blog/lifelong-learning-do-you-know-it-when-you-see-it.

Part I

PROGRAMMING FOR THE OLDER ADULT

CHAPTER I

THE OLDER ADULT POPULATION

Who is the older adult, and what characteristics and life experiences make them different from other adult groups. Historically, this population has been characterized in a negative way as unproductive and dependent on government programs such as Medicare and Social Security. Some of these perceptions are still prevalent as ageism and growing older often show up in the media and workplace (Samuel, 2017, pp. 6–10). However, research shows that there is positive evidence that older adults are capable of learning new things and leading productive lives. That is not to say that there are no physical changes that occur as we age but older adults can and are interested in learning new things, which benefits their mental and physical health. How libraries can use this information in addition to evaluating the needs of the community is discussed in the second half of the chapter as well as ways to create programs that are fun and informative and meet the needs of the older adult population. In the first half of the chapter, I will talk about the generations that make up the older adult population, the aging brain, health, dementia, living arrangements, and technology use.

At what age does the older adult population begin? Medicare can be applied for and used starting at sixty-five years of age. The American Association of Retired Persons (AARP) encourages people who are fifty years and older to sign up for a membership (American Association of Retired Persons, 2019). In 2017, the American Library Association (ALA)—Adult Services Division updated their guidelines for older adults from fifty-five years of age to sixty years and older (Reference and User Services Association [RUSA], 2017). If you ask a baby boomer what age the older population begins, they will tell you seventy-two years of age (Cohn and Taylor, 2010). Recently published books about adult services in the library differ on when the older adult population begins but most generally agree that it begins between fifty-five and sixty-five years of age. The older adult population is a large and diverse group with different cultural and social-economic backgrounds. Though they are a healthier group than previous generations, some, for physical or cognitive reasons, such as injury or disability, may no longer be able to visit the library. For purposes of this book, the older adult is considered anyone who is sixty years of age and older and is unable to visit the library.

A good starting place for understanding the older adult population is to understand the events and experiences that shaped their growing up years. During one of my programs, I played a comedy radio show from the late 1930s. Two of the participants really enjoyed it and laughed. The rest were lukewarm about it. While we were talking, I found out that the two people who enjoyed the radio show had listened to radio shows growing up, while the rest of the group would have watched comedy shows on TV and might have enjoyed watching a clip of a TV show more. You may also find that most of your group was born after 1947 and has little knowledge of World War II or the Korean War, unless they are history buffs, but they may be interested in a program about the Vietnam War. Or they may not like history at all but would enjoy a program about fashion or fads of the time. The point is that there is no one-size-fits-all program for older adults, but if you understand the background, interests, and needs of your audience, then you can create programs that both you and they will enjoy. Let's begin with a discussion of the generations that make up the current older adult population.

GENERATIONS OF THE OLDER ADULT POPULATION

Most people automatically think about the baby boomers when they are asked who the older adult population is. The baby boomer generation is the large and diverse group that includes persons born between 1946 and 1964. Since their birth, they have made an impact on society and still do today. This generation started turning sixty-five in 2011, and they are healthier, working longer, well educated, involved in the community, and interested in learning. The literature is filled with information about this age group and ways to engage them. However, the baby boomers are only one part of the older adult population which libraries may provide programming for.

The older adult population is made up of different generations. Elise Okobi (2014), in her book *Library Services for Adults in the 21st Century,* describes a generation as those born within a certain time span. Each generation experiences the same events and societal changes that shape their beliefs and lifestyle. However, if you look closer, you will find other social-economic and cultural factors that may affect a generation. It is understandable that the focus of programming is on the baby boomer generation, but it is important to remember that there are generations that turned sixty-five before the baby boomers and there will be many generations after the baby boomers who will turn sixty-five (Okobi, 2014; Rothstein, 2010). The older population consists of several generations, and understanding the life events that influenced them is a good starting point when creating programs and services.

From the years 2006–2016, those over age sixty-five increased from 37.2 million to 49.2 million, an increase of 33 percent. That number is expected to increase to 98 million in 2060. Those over eighty-five are expected to double from 6.4 million in 2016 to 14.6 million in 2040, an increase of 129 percent. People reaching one hundred years of age have doubled since 1980.

Increases in immigration have made the U.S. population much more racially and ethnically diverse than it was fifty years ago. In 2016, immigrants accounted for 13.5 percent of the U.S. population. This will impact the makeup of the older adult population as the millennials (the most racially and ethnically diverse generation) enter the older adult population (Lopez and Bialik, 2018).

The current older adult population is made up primarily of three generations followed by two groups who have seen major advancements in technology. The oldest of the older adult population consists of two groups. They have been given many names, but the most common ones are the Greatest Generation and the Silent Generation.

The Greatest or GI Generation

This group was born before 1928 and was given the name the Greatest Generation because they stood up for what was right, often putting other people's needs before their own. They experienced the Great Depression as teenagers and fought in World War II. Research shows that many of them are frugal, trust institutions, value marriage and family, and wish to leave something behind for their children and grand-children. They experienced the transition from silent films to the "talkies" and listened to the music of Louis Armstrong and Tommy Dorsey. In 2019, this generation was ninety-two years and older (Hilton, 2008; Okobi, 2014; Raphelson, 2014; Schroer, 2013).

The Silent Generation

This group was born in the years 1928–1945 and saw many changes in music, technology, and opportunities in education. They were too young to fight in World War II but would have experienced the Great

Depression (or were raised by parents who survived it), the Korean War, the Cold War, and the Space Race. They enjoyed the peace of postwar America at a time when most women stayed at home to raise children and loyalty to a job was most important. They experienced the birth of rock and roll and increased use of television in the home. Research shows that many in this generation are conservative and frugal, take few risks, and familiar activities and environments are important to them. In 2019, this generation was seventy-four to ninety-one years old (Gilton, 2012; Okobi, 2014, p. 5; Schroer, 2013; Shamma, 2011).

Baby Boomers

The baby boomer generation refers to those born between the years 1946 and 1964. They are often talked about as one group who experienced events and societal changes in the same way. However, it does not make sense to compare those who were born in 1946 and fought in the Vietnam War and experienced Woodstock with those born in 1955 who experienced Watergate and the Nixon resignation. Some researchers have begun to look at this generation as two groups, and I have done the same for this discussion.

> ***Baby Boomer I.*** This generation was born in the years 1946–1954, and the oldest of this generation began to turn sixty-five in 2011. Research shows that many are idealistic and educated and question authority. Many major social and political events impacted this group, with the civil rights movement, Woodstock, the Vietnam War, and the assassinations of John F. Kennedy and Martin Luther King being major events in their lives. Many of this generation protested or fought in the Vietnam War, and this standing up for rights continued throughout their life. Those who turned eighteen in 1972 were able to vote with the passage of the Twenty-Sixth Amendment, which lowered the voting age.
>
> This group grew up watching the *Mickey Mouse Club, Gilligan's Island, The Twilight Zone, Star Trek*, and *The Ed Sullivan Show* as well as national news events such as the Kennedy-Nixon debate, the Kennedy funeral, the launching of space shuttles, and the Vietnam War. Music exploded during this time with the rock and roll sound of the Beatles and Motown. Transistor radios were the most used device to listen to music. In 2019, this group was sixty-five years old to seventy-three years old (Hilton, 2008; Okobi, 2014; Schroer, 2013).

> ***Baby Boomer II (sometimes called the Jones Generation).*** The second half of the baby boomer generation was born in the years 1955–1964. This generation may have heard of the Vietnam War, the Kennedy and King assassinations, and the social unrest that the first baby boomers experienced, especially if they had older siblings but would not have participated in the activities associated with these events. This group was the first post–Watergate generation and watched the first walk on the moon. They experienced the oil embargo of 1979 and the Iranian hostage crisis and Nixon's resignation. In the early 1980s, they experienced an economic recession, gasoline shortages, and a tight job market. Heavy metal and hard rock were popular with this generation with the music of Jimi Hendrix, Led Zeppelin, and Queen. This group is college educated and may have had to learn technology as part of their job. As retirement approaches, many in this group will transition to part-time work, volunteering, and pursuing other hobbies they have not had time for. In 2019, this group was between fifty-four years old and sixty-four years old (Hilton, 2008; Okobi, 2014).

Generation X

This generation was born between the years 1965 and 1980. They are the first generation to be called "latchkey kids" as more women were working outside the home, at least part-time. They also experienced their parents' high divorce rates. Research shows that many in this generation tend to experience high levels of skepticism and independence and do not like change. They are highly educated, and a balance between personal life and work is important to them. They experienced the AIDS epidemic, the O.J. Simpson trial, the removal of the Berlin Wall and fall of the Soviet Union, terrorist bombings, and oil tanker spills. This was the first generation to have computers and the Internet as part of their life from an early age. Hip-hop, punk rock, and grunge defined the music of this generation. They came of age with MTV and the emergence of VCRs and Nintendo game consoles. In 2019, this group was thirty-nine years old to fifty-four years old and on the verge of joining the older adult population (Hilton, 2008; Okobi, 2014; Schroer, 2013).

Millennials

The millennials' generation is included in this discussion because they are coming up on the heels of Generation X. As librarians plan ahead for older adult programs and services, they will need to take into account the experiences and needs of upcoming generations. This generation was born in the years 1981–1996. They saw the beginning of the twenty-first century and experienced 9/11, greater security when traveling, the recession of 2008, and the wars in Iraq and Afghanistan. They are college educated with a higher amount of student loan debt than previous generations. This generation is more racially and ethnically diverse than other generations. Research shows that many are more accepting of cultural and ethnic differences, are optimistic about their future, have strong values, and are involved in their community. This group enjoys the music of their older parents and grandparents as well as Coldplay, Red Hot Chili Peppers, Backstreet Boys, Eminem, and rap music. Millennials are wise about technology and grew up with cable TV, the Internet, social media, and streaming services. In 2019, this group was twenty-three years old to thirty-eight years old (Dimock, 2019; Fry, Igielnik, and Patten, 2018; Okobi, 2014; Schroer, 2013; Schull, 2013).

Summary

The older adult population is made up of different generations, each of which experienced similar events in their lives as well as many different social and cultural experiences that shaped them personally. As new generations join the older adult population, they will bring more diversity experiences and skills. An audience at a senior facility may be made up of persons from different generations with different social and cultural experiences. Some may also have physical or cognitive issues, which affect their participation. Library staff may not even know ahead of time who will be participating in an outreach program. Therefore, when creating programs and services, library staff needs to take into account the needs and interests of group. The societal and political events that shaped a generation are a first step in understanding the older adult population, but there are other factors that also need to be considered.

PROFILE OF THE OLDER ADULT

The perception of the older adult as being unproductive and a drain financially on society began early in the twentieth century as longevity and wisdom became less valued. Society turned to the values and the ingenuity of youth, which were appreciated much more. The Older Americans Act of 1965 saw the emergence of the government programs of Medicare and Medicaid along with the expansion of the field of geriatric medicine and the beginning of American Association of Retired Persons. While these were positive advances, they often focused on the problems of aging. In recent years, research has focused on the positive changes that occur as one grows older. While some physical changes are inevitable, the aging brain is capable of learning and changes in lifestyle can slow down the aging process and allow older adults to lead productive lives (Cohen, 2005; Samuel, 2017).

The Aging Brain

The human brain grows rapidly during the first eight years of life, and it was once believed that brain growth peaked in the twenties. However, research shows that this is not true. In fact, the human brain continues to grow throughout life as a result of learning and experience. The body may show signs of aging, with shifts in weight, graying hair, and wearing glasses for close reading, but the brain does not age in the same way.

Brain Mechanics

The human brain weighs about three pounds and has three main parts. The cerebrum, which controls movement, is involved in remembering, solving problems, and emotions. The cerebellum sits under the cerebrum at the back of the head and controls coordination. The third part of the brain is the brain stem, which connects the brain to the spinal cord. The brain stem takes care of things like digestion, heart rate, breathing, and blood pressure. The cortex, which is the outer layer of the cerebrum, specializes in creating and storing memories; processing sights, smells, and sounds; solving problems, and controlling emotions (National Institutes of Health [NIH], 2018).

The brain is made up of billions of cells called "neurons." Sensations, thoughts, memories, emotions, and movements pass through neurons. Simply, when a new image or event is experienced, the brain signals neurons in the brain to make a connection. When an image or event is repeated often, a more permanent connection occurs between the neurons, and new patterns are formed (Cohen, 2005; Jennings, 2018; NIH, 2018; Strauch, 2010).

The human brain is divided into two hemispheres connected with a neural link called the "corpus callosum" and is tasked with handling specialized functions of the brain. For most people the left hemisphere handles speech, language, and problem solving (mathematical and logical reasoning). The right hemisphere specializes in visual, spatial relationships and creativity. While there are variations of how much one hemisphere is used over the other one, research shows that healthy men and women use both hemispheres throughout their lives (Cohen, 2005).

How the Aging Brain Functions

Many parts of the body change as a person ages; however, the brain does not change in the same way as the body unless there has been damage to the neurons. Human beings can and do continue to learn as they age. Some memory loss does occur with age, often in the form of short-term memory. Forgetting why one went to the basement, being easily distracted, or finding it harder to solve problems is all part of aging. Research shows that learning and experience cause positive changes in the brain. The process of taking in stimuli and creating new neural connections in a younger person continues into their old age. By continuing to learn and experiencing new things, the brain continues to grow and reorganize itself. Why there is loss in some areas is not known, but stress, depression, medication, and disease may be factors according to some researchers (Breytspraak and Badura, 2015; Cohen, 2005; Strauch, 2010).

In his research on the aging brain, Cohen (2005) showed that each hemisphere in the brain has specific functions but for older adults the two sides appear to work together to complete a task, recognize a face, recall a word from memory or solve a problem. Scientists compared the brains of young adults and older adults when trying to retrieve a memory using positron emission tomography (PET) scans and magnetic resonance imaging (MRI). When young adults tried to retrieve a memory, they used the left hemisphere. For older adults doing the same activity, they often used both sides of the brain, something called "bilateralization." Though it is not completely understood why this happens, it appears, according to Cohen (2005), that in order to reduce the effects of aging, the right and left hemispheres of a healthy brain have found an efficient and positive way to work together to complete a task. The two hemispheres appear to merge speech and language of the left hemisphere with creativity of the right hemisphere. According to Cohen (2005), writing and storytelling and pursuing other creative outlets is common among older adults: impulses that come about for a variety of psychological and physical reasons and appears to be an example of bi-lateralization (Cohen, 2005; Strauch, 2010).

While there is still more research to be done on the older brain, there are clearly ways to maintain and improve brain fitness and increase quality of life for older adults. Libraries play an important role by providing programs that include involving participants in activities, social interaction, and mastery of a skill.

Creativity and the Brain

Dr. Gene Cohen (2006) took the concept of "bi-lateralization" a step further and studied the influence of creativity on aging. Cohen's study (known as the Creativity Study) was conducted in 2001, in cooperation with the National Endowment of the Arts and the George Washington University. It was one of the first studies to show the positive influence of creativity on aging. The study followed three groups from different parts of the country. The intervention groups were involved in an intensive cultural program led by art professionals, meeting weekly and attending concerts and going to museums. In addition, there was also time allowed for additional art work and practicing. The control groups were also involved in community programs but not intensive programs with professional artists. After a year, the intervention groups showed signs of better health overall and decline in medication use. The experience of mastering a new skill led to feelings of empowerment and a more positive outlook. These phenomena may explain why journaling, storytelling, and literacy programs, which combine books with art projects, are popular library programs for older adults. These types of programs provide participants with an opportunity to be creative, perhaps master a new skill and learn something new, which in turn is beneficial to their health (Cohen, 2005, 2006; National Endowment of the Arts, 2006; Strauch, 2010).

Dementia

"Dementia" is an overall term used to describe a range of symptoms that affect a person's ability to perform everyday activities associated with memory, speech, and perception. There are many types of dementia, but Alzheimer's disease is one of the most common and accounts for 60 to 80 percent of dementia cases. According to the Alzheimer's Association, one in ten Americans aged sixty-five and older have some form of dementia, with 5.8 million Americans living with Alzheimer's disease. In addition, the Alzheimer's Association reports that 50 percent of dementia cases go undiagnosed. The likelihood of getting dementia increases with age, but aging is not the only factor (Alzheimer's Association, 2019d; WebMD, 2016).

While Alzheimer's disease is the most common form of dementia, there are many other forms of dementia. Vascular dementia is the second-most common and often occurs after a stroke. Other conditions can also cause dementia such as thyroid problems and vitamin deficiencies. Some dementia conditions can be reversed. Some conditions resemble dementia, which is why a proper diagnosis is important (Alzheimer's Association, 2019d; WebMD, 2016).

What Is Dementia?

"Dementia" is a term that describes symptoms that are associated with loss of memory and thinking skills and are severe enough to interfere with everyday activities. These changes include a loss of memory and other mental abilities that interfere with daily activities. Dementia isn't simply forgetting someone's name or where you parked. Persons diagnosed with dementia will have problems with at least two of the following (Alzheimer's Association, 2019d; WebMD, 2016):

- Memory
- Language and speech
- Problem solving, concentration, and speech
- Visual perception

Symptoms of Dementia

Dementias other than Alzheimer's often affect other brain sites than memory. Early symptoms of these dementias include problems with language, behavior, mobility, problem solving, and the ability to focus and pay attention. There are many stages of dementia, which range from mild symptoms to the most severe, in which the person is completely dependent on others for care.

Causes of dementia vary depending on what types of brain changes are taking place. Other conditions that resemble dementia-like symptoms can be reversed. Side effects of medication; depression; vitamin deficiencies; thyroid, kidney, or liver problems; and blood clots or tumors can also resemble dementia. Everyone loses neurons as they age; however, people with dementia have greater loss (National Institute on Aging, 2017).

Alzheimer's Disease

Alzheimer's disease is the most common type of dementia. It is increasing in numbers as the older population ages, though it is not caused by aging. It accounts for 60 to 80 percent of dementia cases. It is the sixth leading cause of death in the United States. There is currently no cure for the disease, but some treatments may help treat symptoms in some people. More than sixteen million Americans provide unpaid care for persons diagnosed with Alzheimer's disease (Alzheimer's Association, 2019c; National Institute on Aging, 2017).

What Is Alzheimer's Disease?

Alzheimer's disease is a progressive brain disorder that slowly causes damage to the nerve cells and tissue, throughout the brain, associated with memory and thinking. Research has shown that in the brains of Alzheimer's patients, there is a loss of connection between nerve cells that transmit messages to other parts of the brain and to muscles and organs in the body. The damage appears to begin in the hippocampus, the part of the brain important in forming memories. As the nerve cells die, other parts of the brain are affected. By the final stage of the disease, the brain has shrunk due to the loss of nerve cells, and there is widespread damage that affects communication, recognition of loved ones, and the ability to perform daily tasks (National Institute on Aging, 2017).

Signs and Symptoms

Alzheimer's disease is a progressive brain disease, which can last for years and get worse over time. Research from the Alzheimer's Association and other organizations has shown the difference between normal aging and those which may be early symptoms of Alzheimer's (Alzheimer's Association, 2019b, 2019c; National Institute on Aging, 2017b).

1. An older adult may forget a name or appointment sometimes, but usually they will remember at a later time. Those with Alzheimer's may forget recently learned information and important dates and ask about the same information over and over.
2. Occasional errors in balancing the checkbook or when following a recipe are common in aging adults. Those with Alzheimer's symptoms may have problems following a plan or taking care of monthly bills. They may also have problems concentrating.

3. Needing help with settings on the microwave or help setting up a device to record a television show is a typical aging occurrence. Experiencing problems driving to a familiar location or remembering rules to a favorite game, getting lost easily, and putting items in odd places are early signs of Alzheimer's.

4. Confusion about the day of the week can happen, but many older adults will figure out the correct day later. Those with early Alzheimer's may not remember where they are or how they got there. Losing track of dates, seasons, and time may also occur.

5. Changes in vision are most often due to cataracts. For some people, having problems with reading, judging distance, and determining color or contrast may be a sign of Alzheimer's.

6. Sometimes older adults may have problems finding the right words they want to use in a conversation. However, struggling to join or follow a conversation or stopping midsentence without knowing how to continue is a sign of early Alzheimer's disease.

7. Older adults may lose items occasionally but are usually able to retrace their steps and find them. For those experiencing Alzheimer's, they may not be able to retrace their steps to find an item.

8. Older adults may have specific ways of doing things and become irritable when their routine is changed. They may also occasionally feel tired of work, family, and social activities. Persons with Alzheimer's may have problems keeping up with a favorite sports team or completing a favorite hobby. They may also become confused, suspicious, depressed, or anxious with family or work or when they are not in a familiar setting.

Alzheimer's disease symptoms will get worse over time. In the early stages, persons with early Alzheimer's symptoms may visit the library on their own or with caregivers. It may be hard to detect someone who is experiencing early Alzheimer's disease from someone who is not. In the later stages of Alzheimer's disease, persons may not recognize family members and have trouble speaking, reading, or writing. They may forget daily care activities such as brushing their teeth or combing their hair. In the last stages of the disease, they often live in a residential facility (Alzheimer's Association, 2019b, 2019c; National Institute on Aging, 2017b).

The older adult population is growing, and no doubt libraries are already making changes to meet the needs of this population. Many persons with dementia are perhaps visiting the library on their own or with caregivers. They may exhibit momentary confusion or have problems communicating. In later stages, caregivers may need help in understanding the illness and may be looking for activities or resources for their loved ones. Libraries play an important role in providing a comfortable place for this population. Librarians are not expected to become health professionals, but knowledge about dementia and ways to work with this population is beneficial. In Chapter 7—Mind and Memory—"Understanding Patrons with Dementia," Mary Beth Riedner will discuss how to work with this population and how to create programs for them and their caregivers. Chapter 7 also includes discussion and programs for creating memory cafés and how libraries have become involved in the music and memory program.

Music and Alzheimer's Disease

Researchers over the years have become more interested in understanding the use of music with Alzheimer's patients. Playing music for individuals who have Alzheimer's disease has shown promise in reducing stress and reviving memory. Researchers at the University of Utah examined the brains of a small group of patients with Alzheimer's disease who were given individualized music playlists that were downloaded on to iPods. The results of the study showed that music activates areas of the brain that have not yet been damaged by the disease. Listening to music increased communication among several regions of the brain, which improved mood and communication with staff and family. Although not a cure for Alzheimer's disease and dementia, music may provide an alternative way to work with patients and improve their mood and quality of life (Foster, 2018).

The original Music & Memory program was created by Dan Cohen, who worked with nursing home residents who had Alzheimer's disease. An individualized music playlist was created for each resident and downloaded on to iPods. Residents who used the iPods became more animated and recalled past memories. The *Alive Inside* documentary highlighted the events and results of this program (Music & Memory, 2019). This program has been taken a step further and modified to be used as a library service for patrons. Chapter 7—Mind and Memory—of the Programs section includes outlines from libraries that have implemented this program.

Health and Aging

People are living longer due to better physical and mental health care and education. A child born in 2016 can expect to live until 78.6 years of age, more than thirty years longer than a child born in 1900 (Robinson and Tracy, 2017). Thanks to better water and waste treatment, antibiotics, food inspections, modern dentistry, and vaccinations, less people are dying today from infections, such as pneumonia, flu, tuberculosis, or gastrointestinal illnesses. In 2018, the top causes of death were cardiovascular disease, cancer, stroke, lung disease, and Alzheimer's disease. While older adults are healthier than previous generations, there are lifestyle factors, such as obesity, smoking, and a sedentary lifestyle, that accelerate aging and may require long-term care. The chance of multiple chronic conditions increases with age. Pain, suffering, and disability affect the quality of life of older adults. In 2011, 36 percent of adults sixty-five and older in the United States had some type of disability. Twenty-three percent were impaired in their ability to walk; 9 percent had cognitive disabilities; and 7 percent had visual impairments (Breytspraak and Badura, 2015; Jennings, 2018).

Fortunately for the older population today, there are lifestyle changes and assistive technology that can reduce or aid the effects of aging. Healthy foods, good dental health care, exercise, learning new things, and social interaction promote healthy brain growth and result in a productive life as one grows older (Breytspraak and Badura, 2015; Jennings, 2018).

Living Arrangements

In the twentieth century, an older adult could expect to spend some or all of their last years in a nursing home or senior residential facility. While housing options are changing, in 2017 approximately 5 percent (one in four) of those sixty-five years and older can expect to live in a nursing home, either short term or long term. This number increases with age as does the need for help with personal care. The need for help with personal care for adults eighty five-years and older was 22 percent compared to 9 percent for adults seventy-five to eighty-four and six times for adults' ages sixty-five to seventy-four years or 3 percent (Administration on Aging, 2018).

Housing Options

In a 2012 report by American Association of Retired Persons, nine out of ten older adults preferred to age in place perhaps with outside help. The most cited reasons for aging in place included the desire to remain in a familiar location, convenience, and wanting to be independent. In-home care allows seniors to receive the care they need at home, whether it is basic health checks or an in-home nurse. Families are becoming much more involved with providing in-home care for older family members with chronic conditions. In 2009, 23 percent of the households in the United States had at least one family member who was sixty-five years and older (American Association of Retired Persons, 2012; Breytspraak and Badura, 2015).

The older adult who wishes to move today (or needs to move) has more housing or short-term care opportunities than previous generations. While nursing homes were once the most popular and only option for older adults, retirement communities, home health care, long-term care, assisted living, and adult day care centers are becoming more available. In 2014, in the United States, of the regulated long-term care providers, the majority were residential care communities (45.1 percent), followed by nursing homes (23 percent), home health agencies (18.5 percent), and adult day care centers (7.2 percent). The number of people using nursing home facilities, residential care facilities, or home care services is expected to increase from fifteen to twenty-seven million in 2050 (Administration on Aging, 2018; Harris-Kojetin, Sengupta, Park-Lee, 2016).

Technology

The emergence and adoption of technology is perhaps the biggest divide among the older adult population. How quickly older adults embrace technology depends greatly on whether it was available when they were growing up. Other factors such as income, education, and physical limitations also factor in. While this division will change over time, for the current older adult population, some who have no experience with computers, this is a major issue and one in which the public library can be an important contributor. Statistics of technology use indicates that the older population is embracing technology and sees it as a positive experience, even if they are not adopting it as quickly as those in younger groups. While technology use is higher among the younger adult population, the number of adults sixty-five and up who own a smartphone has increased from 18 percent in 2013 to 42 percent in 2016 (Anderson and Perrin, 2017).

Internet and broadband use has also increased among adults ages sixty-five and older. In the early 2000s, 14 percent of this age group used the internet, and in 2016, 67 percent of this group said that they went online. Use of tablets and e-readers among the older population has also increased. The younger age group of the older population (sixty-five to sixty-nine years) reported in 2016 that 41 percent owned tablets compared with 20 percent of those ages eighty and older. The use of e-readers shows a narrower gap, with 21 percent of those sixty-five to sixty-nine years old and 13 percent of those ages eighty and older owning e-readers (Anderson and Perrin, 2017).

Social media is increasingly being adopted by the older population though again it can be found most used among the younger members of this population. Social media is an important place to find news and information, play games, share experiences and pictures, and connect with friends and family. In 2016, four in ten (40 percent) of the older population under the age of seventy-five years reported ever using social media sites compared with 20 percent of those seventy-five years and older. There are barriers to technology use among the older adults ranging from physical issues to lack of confidence in using technology. Most seniors expressed needing help in using electronic devices. However, once they learned how to use it they used it often and found it to be a positive experience (Anderson, 2017).

Summary

The older adult population is healthier and better educated than previous generations, though they may be faced with lifestyle choices, which may affect mobility and living arrangements. Research has shown that many older adults who do not suffer from damage to the brain can live productive lives. Even if they are less mobile, they can still and often want to continue learning. Stimulation and social interaction are important in living a healthy lifestyle.

Dementia describes a range of symptoms that affect a person's ability to perform everyday activities associated with memory, speech, and perception. There are many types of dementia, but Alzheimer's disease is the most common and accounts for 60 to 80 percent of dementia cases. In the early stages, those with symptoms of Alzheimer's disease may visit the library on their own or with caregivers. In the later stages, family and caregivers may look to the library for information and support. By understanding the needs of this population and working with other agencies in the community, libraries can become a supportive and familiar place for those living with this disease.

Libraries play an important role in their community by recognizing the needs of older adults and providing fun and informational programs including reminiscing programs and computer classes at places where older adults congregate. Not only does this provide a valuable service but it also achieves the library's goal of lifelong learning for the entire community. The next section will discuss techniques that can be used to identify who the nonmobile older adult is in your community.

COMMUNITY AND LIBRARY ASSESSMENTS

Research shows that the older adult population is growing fast and will continue to do so over the next several decades. Many older adults are mobile, but increasingly, there are those who are no longer able to visit the library but would still benefit from the social and cognitive engagement that library programs and services offer. By providing services and programs to older adults, libraries provide a sense of goodwill in the community and also meet their goal of lifelong learning and promotion of reading and literacy. A thorough assessment of the community and your library will provide a profile of this population and those who serve them.

Community Assessment

In an era of accountability and tight budgets, an assessment of the community will provide valuable information about demographics of the older adult population. It can show which groups are not adequately being served by the library and help to identify other organizations that provide similar services. There are many resources that provide detailed information on how to do an assessment of adult services in the library. Many of these techniques have been used to evaluate services and programs in the library; however, some of the techniques can also be used to obtain information about the older adults who are not able to visit the library. Let's first look at where in the community important information can be found.

What Community Information Do You Want to Collect?

- First ask yourself what kind of information you are looking for. Demographic information will identify the size of the adult population and their socioeconomic profile.
- Where is the older adult population living? What housing options are available in your community, and where are they located?
- Are there caregiver groups in the community? Talking with these groups about programs and services the library could offer will provide valuable information for creating programs.
- What other organizations in the community provide services and programs for older adults?

Resources for Obtaining Community Information

There are many resources that will provide statistical information about a community.

- American FactFinder provides statistical information about a community: https://factfinder.census.gov/faces/nav/jsf/pages/index.xhtml
- The U.S. Census, www.census.gov, and the American Community Survey (ACS), https://www.census.gov/programs-surveys/acs/, provide a wealth of information as well as projected population growth.

- Contact state and local agencies responsible for services to the elderly. They often receive and make referrals and will have extensive demographic information.
- Visiting nurses and organizations such as meals on wheels, the local council on aging, American Association of Retired Persons, and caregiver support groups may help in identifying clients who may benefit from library services. They may also provide a place to leave publicity about library services and programs (Bennett-Kapusniak, 2018; Lear, 2013; Roberts, 2012).
- Focus groups may be hard to hold at the library for older adults who are not mobile. Senior agencies and facilities may provide a room where library staff and residents could talk about potential services.

Using the Results of a Community Assessment

An assessment of the community is an integral part of any planning process. It is an ongoing process as patrons and communities change constantly. The information you have collected will help you in planning programs and services for older adults.

- A community assessment will give you demographic information about your community and identify your community's needs. It can also point out groups that may not be served by the library (Roberts, 2018).
- A community assessment will show you how many senior facilities there are in your community and where they are located. Knowing this information allows you to plan how often you can realistically visit each one. Talk to the center administrator about what programs and services the library can offer and what the center's needs are. They may want you to provide programs for residents or perhaps provide a workshop to train staff about creating programs and talk about the resources the library has available.
- A community assessment will give you a list of organizations that have similar priorities and values as the library. Some of the organizations on your list will have in-depth demographic information, which they may be willing to share. They may also be able to identify and reach older adults who would benefit from library services. They will also be valuable resources of expertise from another profession that works with older adults.

Library Assessment

Once you have gathered information about your community, you will want to do an assessment of your library.

- While it may be harder to obtain information about older adults who do not visit the library from library statistics, it is still worthwhile to look at past reports and surveys that have been done. Libraries gather information about their patrons, circulation, programs, and services on a daily basis. These statistics are included in state and local reports, but they can provide baseline data about in-library services and programs and may show what kind of programs have been provided in the community.
- Look at what type of programs/services the library currently offers older adults who do not visit the library. If your library has a history of outreach programming for this population, what programs have been done in the past and how successful were these programs? If you retain old programs, look at what has been done before, and hopefully there will be some comments about how well the program was received or what needed to be done differently.
- Focus groups with activity coordinators and caregivers can help identify older adults who are living at home and what type of services and programs they would benefit from.
- Ask patrons, either verbally or with a short survey, if they have older adults living with them who cannot visit the library. Ask them what services they would like the library to offer.

Summary

An assessment of your community and library will provide important information that can be used to create a plan of action for creating programs and services for older adults who are not able to visit the library. Is the community best served by the library presenting educational and informational programs at a residential facility? Or would a workshop for caregivers and specific program kits to use at home meet the needs of the community's older population? Would it be more effective to work with the local Alzheimer's group to create memory cafés? If you are looking for more information about conducting assessments, here are some resources that provide more detailed information:

Bennett-Kapusniak, Renee K. 2018. *Public Library Programs and Services for Midlife and Beyond.* Santa Barbara, CA: Libraries Unlimited.
Lear, Brett W. 2013. *Adult Programs in the Library.* 2nd ed. Chicago: American Library Association. ALA Editions.
Okobi, Elsie A. R. H. 2014. *Library Services for Adults in the 21st Century.* Santa Barbara, CA: Libraries Unlimited.
Roberts, Ann. 2018. *Designing Adult Services: Strategies for Better Serving Your Community.* Santa Barbara, CA: Libraries Unlimited.
Roberts, Ann, and Stephanie G. Bauman. 2012. *Crash Course in Library Services for Seniors.* Santa Barbara, CA: Libraries Unlimited.

An internal and community assessment has been conducted, and you now have a good understanding of who the nonmobile older adult population is in your community. Your library's mission and goals for this population are clear, and other agencies in your service area that provide services for older adults have been identified. In the next section, I will discuss planning and creating programs for members of the older adult population who are not able to visit the library.

LIBRARY PROGRAMMING

There is no one-size-fits-all programming for older adults. The type of programming and services your library offers will depend on the goals of your library and the needs of older adults in your community. The next section discusses how to approach programming for this group and where to find resources.

Know Yourself

When I first started creating programs to take to senior facilities, I pulled from the skills I learned when I presented toddler and preschool story times years earlier in my career as a youth services librarian. The format I was comfortable with used a variety of materials including books, poetry or audio selections, music, and activities that engaged the audience such as trivia, puzzles, and games. This type of format worked well for me when I started providing programs for older adults living in senior facilities. The children attending toddler and preschool story time were diverse and had different needs. The adult audiences were also diverse and had different needs, so I always made sure I had enough material in case something didn't work and I had to switch to another activity. This format is not for everyone, and as I began my research for this book and collected program outlines, other librarians also talked about capitalizing on your strength. If your strength is art, then create programs that combine books and art. If storytelling is your passion, then include that in your programs. If you are interested in a topic and are having fun, then your audience will too.

Ask yourself if you need more information about working with the older adult population. Would workshops or webinars be beneficial not only for you but perhaps for all staff? Programming resources can be found in many places. An obvious first choice is your own library, which provides books and information in a variety of formats.

In-House Resources

- Start with your own library's collection. The library is a depository of books and information in a variety of formats. This is what separates the library from other organizations. There are books on tape, old radio shows on CDs and DVDs; poetry; short stories; local history; coffee table books and books with large picture and little text; magazines such as *Reminiscence*, which has short stories geared to the older adult; and of course print books. Also don't forget to look at picture books in the juvenile collection. While you want to avoid childish books, there are many stories with wonderful illustrations or photos that would be appropriate for adults.

- Is your library offering computer and e-reader programs in the library that can be modified and used at a senior facility? Older adults who reside in nursing homes or spend time in an adult day care may have a tablet or computer and would be interested in learning how to connect with their family, upload pictures, or find health information. Many libraries are already offering these types of programs and with a few modifications can take them off-site. Chapter 8—"Technology Connections"—of the Programs section offers some innovative technology programs that have been presented off-site.

- Look for free resources on the internet such as trivia questions, quizzes, coloring sheets, and bingo boards.

- Talk with staff about what skills and background they have, and ask them if they would be willing to share their expertise during a senior program. Also, look into the possibility of using volunteers to help with outreach programming.

- Local history. Present your own program supplementing it with information and pictures, found in the history section of the library or the local history society. The Library of Congress also has historical pictures online, which could be used in a program. Ask a member of the local history society to partner with you to present a program.

- Journal and writing programs can be fun, but be aware that some older adults may no longer be able to write or have vision problems. Recording oral histories may be an alternative to this type of program. Roberts (2018, pp. 110–114) provides detailed information about journaling and oral history projects.

- Create program kits that can be checked out and used in a facility by the activity coordinator or for in-home use. These kits could include a variety of themes such as Valentine's Day, road trips, fashion, or be general in nature. The kits would include books, music, DVDs, trivia and games, and some suggestions on how to use the materials.

- Homebound and book delivery services are traditional library services that meet the needs of many non-mobile patrons. But also look at the results of your assessment for older adults who are not using these services but would benefit from a program that gives them an opportunity to interact with others. Are there patrons who live at home with early stage Alzheimer's disease and might benefit from a Music & Memory program? (Refer to the Programs section—Chapter 7.) Would the assisted living facility where you drop off book collections benefit from a literacy and art program?

- Explore grant opportunities that would pay for materials for activity kits or technology. Local or state art council grants may pay for performers or displays. Technology grants may provide "assistive technology loans" to try out potential expensive technology before purchasing (Roberts and Bauman, 2012).

- Create podcasts or tape programs presented in the library, and put it on the library's website so that homebound patrons can access them through their computer or tablet.

- Talk with the organization and/or individual who presented a program at the library about presenting the same program at a senior facility.

- Adapt the summer reading program to the older adult readers unable to visit the library. The activity coordinator can help identify those who would be most interested.

- Libraries also have a lot to offer as well. Libraries have large collections of information and materials that may be useful for training. Many libraries also have meeting rooms and provide a location for workshops for caregivers or memory cafés. If your library has a place for community information, you can suggest that they display their information (Lear, 2013).

CREATING RELATIONSHIPS WITH COMMUNITY ORGANIZATIONS

Once you have identified the organizations and agencies in your community that provide senior services and programs, contact them by email, phone, or a face-to-face meeting, and talk to them about the programs and services they offer. Also take the time to talk about what the library has to offer. Partnerships with other agencies can be beneficial for both the library and the community organization by providing resource sharing, reaching new audiences, providing access to expertise from another profession that works with older adults, and expanding library services and programs beyond what one organization can do on its own. Partnering with another organization may also open up a new site and audience for programs (Lear, 2013).

Community Relationship Options

- Perhaps your library may want to take on the role of a program consultant or provide research information. A workshop about programming for older adults for activity coordinators of senior facilities is one way libraries can extend their services. Libraries are a natural choice for gathering information, finding speakers, setting up a book club, and presenting programs and can offer this information in a training workshop.
- The community assessment may have also provided you with other organizations that may be willing to partner with the library to provide programs such as museums, local history groups, health associations, local symphony or orchestra, the local high school music department, or local colleges or educational institutions (Bennett-Kapusniak, 2018).
- Network with other local libraries and forums such as the Programming Librarian on Facebook and the Programming Librarian Website—www.programminglibrarian.org—and through professional organizations. Find out what others in the profession are doing and what has worked or not worked.

In the past older adults who were not mobile would most likely be found in nursing homes or assisted living. Today, in addition to these, they may be living at home, attending adult day care and memory cafés, or living in senior communities or with a family member. The kind of program or service the library provides will depend on who the audience is and their needs. This next section provides some general suggestions for working with a senior facility and their residents. There is also a discussion of using volunteers for outreach programming.

Connecting with the Senior Facilities

While there is no one-size-fits-all programming, there are some general tips for working with the activity coordinator at a senior facility and the residents as well. Volunteers are also a valuable resource for libraries and can be a beneficial addition to outreach programming.

- Whether this is a first contact with a facility or a follow-up, you will want to talk with the activity coordinator or facility administrator. Before talking to the facility, have an idea of how often you will be able to visit the facility and what days and times work best for the library. Contact the facility activity coordinator by phone or email or set up a face-to-face meeting.

- Jot down their name, title, phone number, and email address for future contact.
- If the library has provided programming at the facility before, ask if these programs met the needs of the facility. What did they like or not like? Are there other ways the library can work with them?
- If this is the first contact, talk about what the library can offer and what has been offered at other facilities. Talk about how often the library can visit the facility and what days and time work best. Describe the type of programs you are thinking about doing, where the group will meet, the equipment the facility has available, and how many people will attend the program. If possible, ask about the skills and abilities of the group.
- Set up a time and date to meet the group. It is okay at this point to take a program that you have used before or take a variety of material with no particular theme to share. Once you have established a relationship with the group, you can find out what they are interested in.
- Be consistent. Decide with the center what date and time and location within the facility you will present programs, and keep to that schedule. It will be easier to remember, and the center can post information about upcoming programs.
- Arrive early to set up equipment and prepare the room. You may not have much control over how the room is set up, but if possible, seating the group at tables or in a semicircle allows for better eye contact and better hearing.
- Greet your audience and talk to them about what you will be presenting. At the end of the program, if you know, tell them what you will be talking about the next time you visit. During the program, take mental notes of what worked, what activities were difficult or fun, and the abilities of the group. After your program, evaluate how the program went. Make notes on what could be added or changed.

Volunteers

Volunteers are a valuable resource for libraries. They shelve library materials, prepare materials for programs, assist in library events, and may deliver book collection to the homebound and senior communities. They can also be valuable resources for outreach programming with supervision and training. Ellsworth Public Library (Programs—Chapter 6—Art-Based Programs) uses volunteers to help residents complete arts-based projects. Carroll County Public Library (Programs—Chapter 8—Technology Connections) uses volunteers to present and participate in their virtual reality programs. The older adult population is healthier and educated, and mobile adults may be looking for something to do with their free time and are very supportive of libraries. They may have an expertise that is fun and informative and would love to help with outreach programs. It is a win-win situation for both.

Many libraries may already have a volunteer policy and program in place that could also be used with outreach program volunteers. This program usually includes a formal application asking for background and experience, background checks, if they are working with residents, and training, evaluations, and formal appreciation recognition. Volunteers are a valuable resource for libraries; however, as Roberts (2018) discusses it is important to find the right person to help with outreach programs. A well-planned and organized volunteer program will ensure that a volunteer is well placed and their time goes smoothly (Bennett-Kapusniak, 2018; Roberts, 2018).

WORKING WITH THE OLDER ADULT POPULATION

- Plan ahead and have plenty of information when you go to a center. If this is the first visit, borrow a program and try it. Once you get to know your audience, use information and resources that meet their needs and that you are comfortable with. Creating a program with lots of activity makes it easier to adapt it to different audiences.

- There can be physical and cognitive barriers when working with this population. If possible, ask the activity coordinator in your initial interview about who your audience will be and what are the abilities and skills of the group. While you may not always know who will be in your group and their skill level may be mixed, you can plan ahead for what you are aware of.

- Arrive early, especially if you have things to set up. Greet your audience and spend time talking to them. If your program is right after lunch, make sure lunch is completed before starting the program.

- Use books with large pictures and illustrations that the audience can see from a distance, such as coffee table books and juvenile (not childish) books with large pictures. If the center has a computer or projector available, create PowerPoint slide shows and use YouTube clips, DVDs, or CDs as part of your program.

- There may be some in your audience who have vision and hearing loss. For visuals use a font size that can be easily seen and read. In my own experience of wearing hearing aids, it is much easier to hear when a person is facing me when talking. Speak clearly, distinctly, and moderately (talking louder or yelling doesn't work). Seat the audience so everyone can see and hear you and each other. Use captions if you are showing something on a DVD. During an activity, you might pair these individuals with a volunteer or another member of the audience to help them complete a task.

- Use assisted devices when needed. If there are people with vision loss, provide magnifiers for them to look at pictures or to read something. The center may have these available for use. If you are doing a journaling program and have participants who have limited use of their hands, you may need to use a recorder or have a volunteer write down their information.

- Crafts have their place and can add an important component to a program. Be aware of your groups' abilities, and prepare ahead the parts that will be difficult. Use volunteers to replace the individual's hands and eyes to complete the craft. At Ellsworth Public Library, volunteers explain what they are doing as they help complete crafts. Consider whether the craft adds to the program or whether a physical activity or trivia game would work better.

CONCLUSION

The older adult population is a diverse group made up of persons from different generations with a variety of backgrounds, interests, and needs. Physical and cognitive problems may keep them away from the library, but their interest in reading and learning may still be strong. This population is larger and will continue to grow over the next several decades. They are faced with more cases of dementia; may struggle with lifestyle choices, which affect their health; have physical impairments, which may require home care or living in a residential facility; and often struggle with technology. Stimulation from activities such as exercise, learning something new, art, music, and interacting with others leads to a more productive life. Unfortunately, this part of the population is often underserved by libraries.

Historically, the older adult population who were not mobile could be found in nursing homes or perhaps living with family members. Today the older adult population has more options available for them and can be found in a variety of locations. If they are still mobile, they may live on their own. If there are physical or cognitive disabilities, they may have live-in care; live with family members, in residential facilities, or assisted care; and attend adult day care or memory cafés. They may visit the library with a caregiver, or caregivers may come to the library for books or information for their loved one.

There is no one-size-fits-all library program for older adults. The traditional services of dropping off book collections at nursing homes and providing homebound services are a great service, which extends the library's primary role of literacy and promoting reading in the community. To meet the goal of lifelong learning and to meet the needs of older adults, libraries need to reach beyond traditional services. Libraries are in a position to offer educational and fun-themed programs that encourage reminiscing and interacting with others. Computer classes, which are a reoccurring class in most libraries, can be taken off-site and used to teach older adults about apps, where to find health information, and how to keep in touch with families and friends. Partnering with other agencies can extend the libraries' services and provide valuable support to patrons who are dealing with a family member who has dementia.

The next section of this book includes a variety of programs from around the country that show how some libraries are creating programs to meet the needs of their older adult population. Information was gathered through email and phone interviews. The programs easily fell into four areas and have been divided into adult story times, art and literacy programs, and memory and technology programs. Each program outline includes a description of the program, supplies needed, and program instructions. For most of the programs, there are also tips/suggestions for working with the older adult population and program variations.

REFERENCES

Administration on Aging. April 2018. "Profile of Older Americans: 2017." Department of Health and Human Services. https://acl.gov/aging-and-disability-in-america/data-and-research/profile-older-Americans.

Alzheimer's Association. 2019a. "Inside the Brain: Part 1: Brain Basics." https://www.alz.org/alzheimers-dementia/what-is-alzheimers/brain_tour.

Alzheimer's Association. 2019b. "10 Early Signs and Symptoms of Alzheimer's." https://www.alz.org/alzheimers-dementia/10_signs.

Alzheimer's Association. 2019c. "2019 Alzheimer's Disease Facts and Figures." https://alz.org/alzheimers-dementia/facts-figures.

Alzheimer's Association. 2019d. "What Is Dementia." https://alz.org/alzheimers-dementia/what-is-dementia.

American Association of Retired Persons. 2012. "Housing an Aging Population: Are We Prepared?" https://www.aarp.org/content/dam/aarp/livable-communities/old-learn/housing/housing-an-aging-population-are-we-prepared-2012-aarp.pdf.

American Association of Retired Persons. 2019. "Membership Services." https://www.aarp.org.

Anderson, Monica, and Andrew Perrin. May 17, 2017. "Tech Adoption Climbs among Older Adults." Pew Research Center. http://www.pewinternet.org/2017/05/17/tech-adoption-climbs-among-older-adults.

Bennett-Kapusniak, Renee K. 2018. *Public Library Programs and Services for Midlife and Beyond*. Santa Barbara, CA: Libraries Unlimited.

Breytspraak, L., and L. Badura. 2015. "Facts on Aging Quiz (Revised from Palmore (1977; 1981)." http://info.umkc.edu/aging/quiz/.

Cohen, Gene D. 2005. *The Mature Mind: The Positive Power of the Aging Brain*. New York: Basic Books.

Cohen, Gene D. Spring 2006. "Research on Creativity and Aging: The Positive Impact of the Arts on Health and Illness." *Generations: Journal of the American Society on Aging*, XXX (no. 1), pp. 7–15. https://www.agingkingcounty.org/wp-content/uploads/sites/185/2016/07/RESEARCH-ON-CREATIVITY-AND-AGING.pdf.

Cohn, D'Vera Cohn, and Paul Taylor. December 20, 2010. "Baby Boomers Approach 65—Glumly." Pew Social Trends. http://www.pewsocialtrends.org/2010/12/20/baby-boomers-approach-65-glumly.

Dimock, Michael. January 17, 2019. "Defining Generations: Where Millennials End and Generation Z begins." Pew Research Center. https://www.pewresearch.org/fact-tank/2019/01/17/where-millennials-end-and-generation-z-begins/.

Foster, Norman. April 27, 2018. "Music Activates Regions of the Brain Spared by Alzheimer's Disease." University of Utah Health Department. https://healthcare.utah.edu/publicaffairs/news/2018/04/alzheimer.php.

Fry, Richard, Ruth Igielnik, and Eileen Patten. September 9, 2018. "How Millennials Today Compare with Their Grandparents 50 Years Ago." Pew Research Center. http://www.pewresearch.org/fact-tank/2018/03/16/How-Millennials-Compare-With-Their-Grandparents/.

Gilton, Donna L. 2012. *Lifelong Learning in Public Libraries: Principles, Programs and People*. Lanham, MD: Scarecrow Press, Inc., 194–196.

Harris-Kojetin, L., M. Sengupta, E. Park-Lee, et al. 2016. "Long-Term Care Providers and Services in the United States: Data from the National Study of Long-Term Care Providers, 2013–2014." National Center for Health Statistics. Vital Health Statistics 3(38). https://www.cdc.gov/nchs/data/series/sr_03/sr03_038.pdf.

Hilton, Robin. June 6, 2008. "The Sound of a Generation." NPR: *All Songs Considered.* www.npr.org/sections/allsongs/2008/06/the_sound_of_a_generation.html.

Jennings, Timothy R. 2013. *The Aging Brain: Proven Steps to Prevent Dementia and Sharpen Your Mind.* Grand Rapids, MI: Baker Books, 2018, 15–30.

Lear, Brett W. 2013. *Adult Programs in the Library.* 2nd ed. Chicago: American Library Association.

Lopez, Gustavo, and Kristen Bialik. November 20, 2018. "Key Findings about U.S. Immigrants." Pew Research Center: Fact Tank. http://www.pewresearch.org/fact-tank/2018/11/30/key-findings-about-u-s-immigrants/.

Mayo Clinic. February 24, 2018. "Alzheimer's and Dementia: What's the Difference." https://www.mayoclinic.org/diseases-conditions/alzheimers-disease/expert-answers/alzheimers-and-dementia-whats-the-difference/faq-20396861.

Music & Memory. 2019. "Mission and Vision." https://musicandmemory.org/about/mission-and-vision/.

National Endowment of the Arts. April 2006. "The Creativity and Aging Study: The Impact of Professionally Conducted Cultural Programs on Older Adults, the Final Report." https://www.arts.gov/sites/default/files/NEA-Creativity-and-Aging-Cohen-study.pdf.

National Institutes of Health. December 2018. "Brain Basics: Know Your Brain." https://www.ninds.nih.gov/Disorders/Patient-Caregiver-Education/Know-Your-Brain.

National Institute on Aging. 2017a. "Basics of Alzheimer's Disease and Dementia: What Is Dementia? Symptoms, Types, and Diagnosis." https://www.nia.nih.gov/health/what-dementia-symptoms-types-and-diagnosis.

National Institute on Aging. May 17, 2017b. "Memory and Thinking: What's Normal and What's Not?" U.S. Department of Health & Human Services. https://www.nia.nih.gov/health/cognitive-health.

Okobi, Elise A. R. H. 2014. *Library Services for Adults in the 21st Century.* Santa Barbara, CA: Libraries Unlimited.

Raphelson, Samantha. October 6, 2014. "From GIs to GenZ (or Is It iGen?): How Generations Get Nicknames." National Public Radio (NPR). https://www.npr.org/2014/10/06/349316543/don-t-label-me-origins-of-generational-names-and-why-we-use-them.

Reference and User Services Association (RUSA). September 2017. "Guidelines for Library Services with 60+ Audiences: Best Practices." http://www.ala.org/rusa/sites/ala.org.rusa/files/content/resources/guidelines/60plusGuidelines2017.pdf.

Roberts, Ann. 2018. *Designing Adult Services: Strategies for Better Serving Your Community.* Santa Barbara, CA: Libraries Unlimited, pp. 103–109.

Roberts, Ann, and Stephanie G. Bauman. 2012. *Crash Course in Library Services for Seniors.* Santa Barbara, CA: Libraries Unlimited.

Robinson, Kristen and Kristen Tracy. July 25, 2017. "Reflecting on the Profile of Older Americans, Senior Corps: 'Tuesday Talks.'" Corporation for National and Community Service. https://www.nationalservice.gov/sites/default/files/upload/Tuesday%20Talks%20-%20Profile%20of%20Older%20Americans%20v3.pdf.

Rothstein, Pauline, ed. 2010. *Boomers and Beyond: Reconsidering the Role of Libraries.* Chicago: American Library Association, pp. 3–21.

Samuel, Lawrence R. 2017. *Aging in America.* Philadelphia: University of Pennsylvania Press, pp. 6–10.

Schroer, William J. 2013. "Generation X, Y, Z and the Others." WJS Marketing. http://socialmarketing.org/archives/generations-xy-z-and-the-others/.

Schull, Diantha D. 2013. *50+ Library Services: Innovation in Action.* Chicago: American Library Association.

Shamma, Rasnim. November 4, 2011. "What's the Defining Moment of Your Generation?" National Public Radio (NPR). https://www.npr.org/2011/11/02/141930849/whats-the-defining-moment-of-your-generation.

Strauch, Barbara 2010. *The Secret Life of the Grown-Up Brain.* New York: Penguin Publishing.

WebMD. December 26, 2016. "Alzheimer's and Dementia: What Is the Difference?" https://www.webmd.com/alzheimers/guide/alzheimers-and-dementia-whats-the-difference#1.

PART II

THE PROGRAMS

Programs for older adults are varied and presented in different formats and styles. There is no one right way to program, which is why it is important to understand the needs and interests of the older adults you are providing programs for. There are over thirty programs discussed in this part that have been created by me and other adult services library staff around the United States for use with older adults who are not able to visit the library. The program information was taken from phone interviews and email correspondence.

As I began to talk with other librarians about their programs, I found that these programs fit into four areas—traditional story times, crafts and literacy, memory and mind programs, and technology programs. The programs are meant to be informational, fun, and creative and provide an opportunity for older adults to interact and reminisce with one another. Most of the programs include a description, supplies and materials needed, program instructions, tips/suggestions for working with older adults, and program variations. Some of the programs have been presented in a library setting, and there are suggestions on how to modify them for use off-site.

The first four chapters of Part II contain programs that are considered adult story times. These programs are built around a theme and include activities that encourage reminiscing and having fun while interacting with others. They include stories, activities, trivia, music, games, and sometimes a craft. These programs can be modified depending on the interests and needs of the groups. Chapter 6 includes programs that involve creating a craft project by itself or combining the creativity of crafts with literature.

Chapters 7 and 8 focus on two issues that older adults face. Research has shown that as the older adults age, so does the possibility of having dementia or Alzheimer's disease. As libraries begin to expand adult programming to older adults outside of the library, they may need to offer programs for residents with early-stage dementia or Alzheimer's. Chapter 7 begins with a discussion by Mary Beth Riedner, retired librarian and creator of the Tales and Travels program, about the stages of dementia and Alzheimer's disease with suggestions for working with this population. Included in Chapter 7 are a variety of programs that have been used to address this need.

The emergence of technology has created a division among the current older adult population. While more information is found online, a large proportion of the older adult population does not feel confident using technology, if they even own it. Research has shown that once adults are shown how to use technology, they feel more confident using it and consider it a positive experience. Most libraries are already providing in-house technology programs and with a few modifications can provide these programs off-site.

In Chapter 8, Adam Chang, the instruction and research librarian at Central Ridge Library, Florida, begins the discussion of technology connections with information on how to conduct computer classes without a dedicated computer lab. Delray Beach Public Library staff used these same techniques to create their Appy Hour computer programs. While the program was originally presented in the library, they discuss ways to modify this program for use at senior facilities. Carroll County Public Library staff has had success with using virtual reality in outreach programs, which they share in this chapter, and staff at the Missoula Public Library in Montana share a description of their mobile computer lab, which delivers computer classes on wheels.

These programs are examples of successful programs library staff around the country have presented to older adults. They can be taken to senior residential facilities, adult day care, memory cafés, and assisted living facilities or used in the library. These programs can be used as is or as a springboard to creating other programs.

Information about the following programs was gathered from phone interviews and e-mail correspondence with the following librarians and used with their permission:

Jennifer Baugh, Six Mile Regional Library District

Jennifer Bishop, Carroll County Public Library

Barbara Brown, Peoria Public Library

Marie Corbitt, Westerville Public Library

Carlye Dennis, Fayetteville Public Library

Mary Fahndrich, Madison Public Library

Julie Hyland, Wisconsin Music & Memory Program

Jackson District Public Library

Mary Kay Johnson, Norwalk Easter Public Library

Valerie Lewis, Suffolk Cooperative Library System

Alyson Low, Fayetteville Public Library

Stacey McKim, Iowa City Public Library

Loanis Menendez, Delray Beach Public Library

Tiffany Meyer, Ellsworth Public Library

Angela Meyers, Bridges Library System

Missoula Public Library

Cari Pierce, Peoria Public Library

Dorothy Stoltz, Carroll County Public Library

Alyson Walzer, Delray Beach Public Library

Judith Wright, Homewood Public Library

CHAPTER 2

JUST FOR FUN

INTRODUCTION

Reminiscing about past experiences, interacting with others, and laughing are beneficial to an individual's health and well-being. The programs in this chapter are meant to be fun and provide an opportunity to talk about past trends and experiences. While two of the programs present an opportunity to reminisce about candy enjoyed while growing up and special pets, the humor program also provides a time to laugh and enjoy jokes, funny headlines, and stories. This format can also be used with other fun topics, so think outside the box and talk to your group about their interests.

Each program outline includes a description of the program and supplies that are needed. There are discussion questions, and an outline of the program activities included. Suggestions and tips for working with older adults and additional activities are also included.

LET'S HAVE A GOOD LAUGH

Program by Phyllis Goodman

Description

April is National Humor Month, officially, but anytime of the year is good for a program that includes funny stories, laughter, and humor. This program includes a discussion about the pranks participants played on others when they were young and the jokes they enjoy now. If possible, bring in some pranks—snakes in a can, Whoopee cushion, hand buzzer, and so on—to show and pass around. This program includes humorous stories, trivia, and comedy shows that may have been listened to on the radio or watched on TV.

Supplies/Materials Needed

- Jokes, funny one-liners, or newspaper headlines. (Look in the 818.6 section of the library collection for joke books and humorous writings.)
- Props: whoopee cushion, hand buzzer, snake in a can, laughing tracks, or other fun gags.

  Norman Rockwell's April Fools' *Saturday Evening Post* Covers—The Game—1943, Fishing—1945, and Curiosity Shop—1948 (information from ElderSong Publications Inc., newsletter, 2013).
- Carol Burnett or Red Skelton comedy show on DVD.
- Book—*If Life Is a Bowl of Cherries, What Am I Doing in the Pits?* by Erma Bombeck.
- Small washboards and other everyday items such as spoons, piece of wood, pie pans with rubber bands.

Program Instructions

1. Arrive early to set up the room and equipment. Greet the participants as they enter the room or finish up a previous activity.

2. Introduce the theme of the program, and begin by asking participants questions to engage them in discussion, such as the following:

   a. What pranks or gags do you remember playing on others when you were younger?

   b. Do you have any favorite jokes?

   c. What makes you laugh?

3. Take out one gag/prank item at a time and demonstrate how it works. Allow participants to try them if they wish to.

4. Share jokes and funny newspaper headlines. Joke books can be found in the library collection, and funny newspaper headlines, such as Jay Leno's funny headlines, can be found online. Prepare the headlines in advance by typing them in a large font on cardstock and laminating, or create a PowerPoint slide show of the headlines.

5. Create a list of famous one-liners ahead of the program. Famous one-liners can also be found on the Internet. Read the line to the audience, and have them guess who said it or what movie it is from.

6. Read a passage from Erma Bombeck's book, *If Life Is a Bowl of Cherries, What Am I Doing in the Pits?*

7. In the 1940s, Norman Rockwell created three April Fool paintings that included many errors. The covers include The Game—1943; Fishing—1945; and Curiosity Shop—1948. These covers can be found online and can be printed out and laminated or saved to a flash drive and shown on a monitor. Show the covers, one at a time, and have the audience point out where the errors are.

From *On the Go with Senior Services: Library Programs for Any Time and Any Place* by Phyllis Goodman.
Santa Barbara, CA: Libraries Unlimited. Copyright © 2020.

8. After everyone has had a chance to look at the picture, point out some of the errors missed (Elder-Song Publications Inc., 2013). The errors for all three covers by Norman Rockwell can be found at http://www.saturdayeveningpost.com/2010/09/22/art-entertainment/norman-rockwell-art-entertainment/rockwell-april1.html.

9. Play a DVD or YouTube clip of a comedy show such as Bob Hope, Carol Burnett, or Red Skelton's shows.

10. Hand out washboards and other everyday things such as a piece of wood, spoons, pie pans with rubber bands to create some fun music.

Suggestions/Tips for Interacting with Residents

- Ask questions throughout the program to encourage participants to share and reminisce.
- If possible, have participants sit around tables. It will make it easier for the washboard band. Encourage everyone to participate, but if someone is not interested, encourage them to stay and enjoy the music.
- Use a large font for any text that you want the group to read, or create the material on a PowerPoint slide and enlarge the font as needed.
- Have magnifiers available for those with vision problems to use while looking at the Norman Rockwell covers.

Program Variations

- Check the library's DVD and audiobook collection for comedy and radio shows. Silent movies are also another excellent option.
- There are several podcasts that may work well and be short enough, such as National Public Radio's (NPR) *Wait, Wait Don't Tell Me*, and *Comedy of the Week*.
- Check your library collection for other authors who write humorous stories, including Erma Bombeck, Robert Fulghum, Bailey White, and Garrison Keillor.

REFERENCES

ElderSong Publications, Inc. March 1, 2013. "Funny Days Activity Newsletter," blog. https://blog.eldersong.com/2013/03/whats-so-funny.

Saturday Evening Post. September 22, 2010. "Answers to Rockwell's April Fools Covers." http://www.saturdayeveningpost.com/2010/09/22/art-entertainment/norman-rockwell-art-entertainment/rockwell-april1.html.

PETS

Program by Phyllis Goodman

Description

Pets are an important part of family life. As children, a cat, dog, fish, guinea pig, or parrot may have been an important part of the family. New pets enter our lives as we marry and start families also. The stories and memories of the pets in one's life are important, and this program gives older adults an opportunity to talk about their pets and reminisce. This program also includes trivia and information about famous pets in TV and literature and music.

Supplies/Materials Needed

- Pictures of famous pets from literature, movies, and TV
- *Old Possum's Book of Practical Cats* by T. S. Eliot
- Cats musical soundtrack by Andrew Lloyd Webber—song "Naming of the Cats"
- *Chicken Soup for the Cat & Dog Lover's Soul*: celebrating pets as family with stories about cats, dogs, and other critters by Jack Canfield.

Program Instructions

1. Arrive early to set up the room and equipment. Greet the participants as they enter the room or finish up a previous activity.

2. Introduce the theme, and ask participants questions about pets they had growing up. Try some of these questions to begin the discussion:

   a. Did you ever have a pet when you were younger? What type of pet did you have?

   b. Were you responsible for taking care of your pet?

   c. Was your pet a good companion?

   d. What did you like to do together?

   e. What was the name of your pet? Were you the one who named it?

   f. Did your pet sleep in your room?

   g. Did you take your pet on trips with you?

3. Read the "Naming of the Cats" from *Old Possum's Book of Practical Cats* by T. S. Eliot.

   Option: Play the song "Naming of the Cats" from the *Cats* album by Andrew Lloyd Webber. Type the lyrics in large font on poster board or display on the computer so the participants can follow along.

4. Read a selection from *Chicken Soup for the Cat & Dog Lover's Soul* by Jack Canfield.

5. If time allows, read some more poems from *Old Possum's Book of Practical Cats* by T. S. Eliot, or play more songs from the Broadway show *Cats* by Andrew Lloyd Webber.

6. Discuss famous pets from literature, movies, and TV. Research famous TV, movie, and books for real famous pets, and prepare pictures ahead of time. Save pictures on a flash drive, create a slide show, or print onto cardstock and pass around.

7. Ask the participants what the name of the pet is and what TV show, movie, book, or famous person the pet belonged to. Another way to do this activity is to give the name of the show or movie and ask the

group what the name of the pet is. Share some trivia about the pet (information sources used for this activity: Castle, 2017; Harrison, 2017).

Famous TV/Movie Pets

a. **Lassie**—TV show (1954–1973). Lassie was played by multiple male collies. The original collie was named Pal, and several of his offspring played the part. Lassie's first human companion was Jeff Miller and then Timmy Martin in the fourth season.

b. **Toto**—*Wizard of Oz*, movie—1939. Toto, a cairn terrier, was Dorothy's pet in the *Wizard of Oz*. Her real name was Terry, but she was later renamed Toto.

c. **Mr. Ed**—TV (1961–1966). Sitcom about a horse who talked only to his owner, Wilbur.

d. **Elvis**—*Miami Vice* TV show (1984–1990). Elvis was a drug-sniffing alligator owned by detective James "Sonny" Crockett.

e. **Flipper**—TV show (1964–1967). Rescue dolphin that assisted his owner Porter Ricks, ranger of Coral Key Park, Florida.

f. **Socks**—President Clinton's family pet. As a cartoon avatar, Socks guided visitors through the White House on the official White House website.

g. **Hedwig**—Harry Potter series. Harry received Hedwig from Hagrid as a birthday gift.

h. **Wilbur**—*Charlotte's Web*—a children's chapter book published in 1952. This is the story of a special friendship between a barn spider, named Charlotte, who writes messages in her spider web to save Wilbur, the pig, from being killed.

i. **Cujo**—a dog in Stephen King's book and movie by the same name. Cujo is a St. Bernard who gets rabies and terrorizes the community. In the movie, five different St. Bernards, one mechanical dog head and a person wearing a costume, were used.

j. **Silver**—*The Lone Ranger* TV show (1949–1957). Silver, a wild stallion, became the Lone Ranger's sidekick after he was rescued from a buffalo herd.

k. **Marley**—a loving and mischievous dog whose life is depicted in the memoir called *Marley & Me* by John Grogan (2005). It was also made into a movie starring Jennifer Aniston and Owen Wilson.

l. **Dino**—*Flintstones* TV show (1960–1966). Dino was a Snorkasaurus who became the family pet after following Fred home from work.

m. **Odie**—Garfield's sidekick. Odie was on a car dealership commercial. Odie appeared in Jim Davis's *Garfield* cartoon books, comic strips, and TV shows.

n. **Fred**—*Baretta* TV show (1975–1978). Fred was the pet cockatoo owned by Tony Baretta, who was a New York City detective. Fred originally spoke Chinese and had to learn English.

o. **Eddie**—dog on *Frasier* TV show (1993–2004). Eddie was played by two Jack Russell Terriers named Moose and his son Enzo.

Suggestions/Tips for Interacting with Residents

- Encourage all in the audience to participate, but respect that they may not want to. Encourage them to stay and listen.
- Use a large font and large, clear pictures for items you wish to show or have participants read.

Program Variations

- Show some YouTube funny videos about pets or pet food advertisements.
- Instead of famous pets trivia, create a trivia quiz using interesting facts about dogs and cats.
- Dog and cat idioms. Talk about some of the sayings about cats and dogs and what they mean. For instance, "dog days of summer" means the hot days of summer. What other idioms can the group come up with?
- Share one or two stories from National Public Radio's (NPR) *Driveway Moments: Dog Tales* and National Public Radio's (NPR) *Driveway Moments: Cat Tales.*
- Share other books about animals/pets, such as *All Creatures Great and Small* by James Herriot, *Marley & Me* by John Grogan, *The Art of Racing in the Rain* by Garth Stein, *Seabiscuit* by Laura Hillenbrand, or *A Street Cat Named Bob* by James Bowen.

REFERENCES

Castle, Alyssa. July 14, 2017. "12 Most Famous Dogs from Movies and TV." Zoomer. http://www.everythingzoomer .com/arts-entertainment/2017/07/14/famous-dogs-from-movies-and-tv/.
Harrison, Shaun. July 14, 2017. "The Greatest TV Pets." TV Guide. http://www.everythingzoomer.com/ arts-entertainment/2017/07/14/famous-dogs-from-movies-and-tv/.

THE SWEET TASTE OF CANDY AND CHOCOLATE

Program by Phyllis Goodman

Description

For many candy and chocolate lovers, a sweet treat is something that was enjoyed as a child and, when possible, enjoyed as an adult. They may have saved their allowance or earned money to visit the local candy store. This program includes some fun facts and history about candy and chocolate, games, trivia, and a book talk from Nancy Coco's books from the *Candy Coated* series.

Supplies/Materials Needed

- History and fun facts about candy.
- PowerPoint slide show showing the history of chocolate and popular candy.
- *Candy Coated* series by Nancy Coco.
- *Willie Wonka & the Chocolate Factory* DVD.
- Samples of candy/chocolate. Prearrange with the center.

Program Instructions

1. Arrive early to set up the room and equipment. Greet the participants as they enter the room or finish up a previous activity.
2. Seat the residents in a circle or around a table so they can see the slide show. Prepare the slides so that the photos are large and clear enough to see. Use a large font for text on the slide, and keep the information brief. Speak in a clear voice, and check once in a while that the audience can hear you.
3. Introduce the theme, and ask the audience what their favorite candy was when they were growing up. These are some other questions to encourage discussion:
   a. Was there a neighborhood candy store where you purchased candy? Were you allowed to go there by yourself?
   b. Did you use your allowance to buy candy?
   c. Have you ever received candy as a gift? What occasion?
   d. Have you ever gone to Cracker Barrel, Jungle Jim's, Dylan's Candy store, or a candy store in your town?
4. Display candy wrappers, or pass them around and ask if anyone had ever tried them.
5. Discuss or share a passage from one of Nancy Coco's *Candy Coated* mystery series.

   The mystery series consists of several books set in a fudge shop in a historic hotel on Mackinac Island in northern Michigan. Each book contains a mystery that is neatly solved by the end of the book and a recipe for fudge.
6. Play the Candy Slogan game. Create a PowerPoint slide show, with each slide showing a slogan for a particular candy. Or print the slogans in a large font onto cardstock and laminate. Hold the slogan boards up, or pass them around. Ask the group if anyone knows what candy the slogan is referring to. For instance, "the milk chocolate melts in your mouth, not in your hand." Answer: M&M's. For fun, keep track of how many correct answers there are. Sporcle and the Candy Addict websites both have lists of candy slogans (Candy Slogans and Jingles, 2006; Candy Slogans Quiz Stats, 2014).

7. History of candy and chocolate. Create a PowerPoint slide show with some fun facts about candy and chocolate (information sources used for the slide show: Cadbury, 2010; Candy History and Origins, 2018; Fun Facts about Candy, 2018; Lacey, 2013; Lauren, 2010; Troy, 2012; Tucker, 2019).

   a. In the Roman, Greek, and Egyptian cultures, fruits and nuts were dipped in honey. As sugar became more popular in the Middle Ages, upper-class Europeans enjoyed sweet treats. It was thought that sugar had medicinal powers and was used to heal the body. Sugar was found to preserve fruit and was later used to make jams and jellies.

   b. The Mayan and Aztec cultures grew cacao trees and used the beans as money. Cacao beans were also roasted and mixed with chili and peppers to make a bitter drink for the king and members of the court. Cacao and eventually chocolate made its way to Spain when Spanish explorers returned home.

   c. In the early 1800s, sugar was more available and less expensive. Candies mixed with fruit, lollipops, taffy pulls, and penny candies were also very popular. By the mid-1800s, there were over 350 candy factories in the United States. The first chocolate factory, Walter Baker & Company, was built in 1765 in Massachusetts.

   d. These are some of the names of those early companies though many have been bought out by larger companies or have disappeared. Do you recognize their name and/or product?

   Fred W. Amend in Chicago—Chuckles, 1921 (eventually purchased by Hershey).

   Tootsie Roll—Tootsie Pop, Dots, 1972; Blow Pops, 1988; Sugar Babies and Sugar Daddy, Double Bubble Gum, and Andes Mints, 1993.

   Welch—James Welch created Junior Mints, which are still sold by Tootsie Roll.

   Curtis—Chicago, founded in 1916—Baby Ruth and Butterfinger.

   Holloway—Milk Duds, Slo-Pokes, and Black Cows.

   Hollywood—Zero Bar, Pay Day, Milk Shake.

   Ludens—known for its cough drops and candy bars—Mellow mints, 5th Avenue bar, and Super Nut.

   Ferrara Pan—Red Hots, 1930s; Cinnamon Jawbreaker, Atomic Fireball, Boston Baked Beans, Lemon Head, 1954.

   Peter Paul—Mounds, Almond Joy, Caravelle bar, 1966; York Peppermint Pattie, 1972; bought by Hershey in 1988 to manufacture and distribute items in the United States.

   Sunline—Pixy Stix, 1952; Bottle Caps, 1972; and Sweet Tarts and Spree; bought by the Nestle Company in 1988.

   e. NECCO wafers were the first mass-produced candy in the United States. They were made by the New England Confectionary Company in Boston though it did not become a company until the early 1900s. The wafers came in different flavors, including peppermint, chocolate, cinnamon, wintergreen, and lemon. They are also known for their conversation hearts, Clark bars, Mary Janes, Candy Buttons, the Sky Bar, and Havilland Candy. In 2018, the NECCO wafer and conversation hearts were bought by the Spangler Candy Company of Ohio.

   f. In 1847, Joseph Fry found a way to mix cocoa powder and sugar into a paste, which was then pressed into a mold. Fry's Chocolate factory began making the Fry's Chocolate Cream bar in 1866. In 1849, John Cadbury made a similar product, but both his bar and Fry's bar were very bitter. Henry Nestle in 1875, creator of evaporated milk, created a tastier chocolate bar by combining chocolate and condensed milk.

   g. Ghirardelli was created in 1849 during the San Francisco gold rush. It was known for the foil-wrapped candy tubes called flicks, which were popular at the movies. It was bought by Quaker Oats in the 1970s, which invested money in the *Willy Wonka* movie to promote its Wonka candy line.

h. The candy industry was at its peak from the 1950s through the 1980s partially due to the return of World War II soldiers, who had tasted chocolate during the war and wanted to continue enjoying and sharing it with their families.

i. **The Hershey Company**—located in Hershey, Pennsylvania—created the Hershey candy bar that reached store shelves in 1900, followed by the Hershey kisses in 1907 and the Hershey bar with almonds in 1908. The Reese's Peanut Butter Cup was introduced in 1923 by Harry B. Reese, a Hershey employee who wished to start his own company while using Hershey chocolate. In 1963 Reese's was bought by the Hershey Company. Hershey is also known for its Mr. Good bar, the Krackel bar, and Chuckles. Today Hershey is one of the largest chocolate companies in the world.

j. **Nestle Company** created a tasty chocolate bar in 1875. It was located originally in Switzerland, and in 1899 Nestle obtained land for a chocolate manufacturing plant in Fulton, New York. From then on, Nestle became a staple in the American home, many of which enjoyed its Nestle Quik and chocolate chips.

k. **Mars Company**—Frank C. Mars started selling chocolate from his home in Tacoma, Washington, in the early 1900s. After several setbacks, he created the Milky Way bar in 1923, which was different from other candy items on the market. It was created as a competitor to the malted milkshake rather than the Milky Way galaxy in space, as was believed. The Snickers bar followed in 1930, adding peanuts and caramel. The Three Musketeers followed in 1932, with fluffy chocolate nougat in vanilla, strawberry, and chocolate. In 1936, the Forever Yours bar was created.

l. In the 1930s, Forrest Mars, with his father's money and the Milky Way recipes, went to England to open a candy business. It was very successful, and eventually he bought out his father and created M&Ms.

m. **M&Ms Candy**—The idea for M&Ms came from rations soldiers were given, which included small bites of chocolate that did not melt. Forrest Mars and Bruce Murrie, son of the 1940 president of the Hershey Company, formed a partnership to make M&Ms. M&Ms, which used Hershey's chocolate, was covered in a candy shell. The candy was introduced in 1954 and called M&M after Mars's two sons. In 1854 peanut M&Ms were introduced. The original colors of the candy were red, brown, yellow, green, and violet. The color red was discontinued in the 1970s due to health concerns about the dye.

n. **Movie Candy**—Buying candy to eat at a movie is as popular today as it was in the past. Drive-in movie theaters were popular in the 1960s and continued until the 1980s. The candy treat during a movie had to be bite size, to be able to be eaten quietly, and to last a long time. Popular movie candy included M&Ms, Raisinets, Sno-Caps, Bit-o-Honey, Junior Mints, Starburst, Skittles, Licorice, Good & Plenty, and Milk Duds.

o. **TV advertisements**—In the 1950s and 1960s, TV candy companies advertised on popular children's TV shows such as *Howdy Doody* and the *Mickey Mouse Club*. TV sit-cons and sports players also partnered with the candy companies.

p. William Morrison invented cotton candy, which was originally called fairy floss.

q. There are also a large variety of caramels, taffy, mellow crèmes, licorice, jawbreakers, and suckers. Chicago's M. J. Holloway not only made Milk Duds but also Slo-Pokes and Black Cows. Walnettos were introduced by Minnesota's J. N. Collins Company in 1919 and was one of the most popular candies during World War II. Walnettos was mentioned during a laugh-in skit (1967–1973) where the old man tried to pick up a woman on a park bench. When nothing else worked, he tried, "How about a Walnetto?"

8. If permitted, share some different candies with the participants.

Suggestions/Tips for Interacting with Residents

- Bring in some candy or sugar-free candy for all to taste. Check with the activity coordinator about special diets beforehand.
- During the slide show, make sure the audience can hear you and see the slides.
- Ask questions throughout the program to keep the conversation going. Don't worry if the conversation gets sidetracked. The side conversations are sometimes the best part of the program.

Program Variations

- Some of the American candy factories have stores and websites, such as Jelly Belly, Spangler, Doscher's Candies, Fannie May, and Hershey. Check to see if they have a virtual reality tour.
- Play some candy commercial clips from YouTube.

REFERENCES

Cadbury, Deborah. 2011. *Chocolate Wars: The 150-Year Rivalry between the World's Greatest Chocolate Makers.* New York: Perseus Books Group.

"Candy History and Origins." 2018. http://www.candyhistory.net/candy-origin/.

"Candy Slogans and Jingles." March 5, 2006. Blog. https://candyaddict.com/blog/2006/03/05/candy-slogans-and-jingles/.

"Candy Slogans Quiz Stats." September 15, 2014. https://www.sporcle.com/games/g/candyslogans.

"Fun Facts about Candy." 2018. http://www.candyhistory.net/candy-facts/candy-fun-facts/.

Lacey, Darlene. 2013. *Classic Candy.* Oxford, United Kingdom: Shire Publications.

Lauren, Dylan. 2010. *Dylan's Candy Bar: Unwrap Your Sweet Life.* New York: Clarkson Potter.

Troy, Eric. September 12, 2012. "Culinary Lore: Food Science, History, and Much More." https://culinarylore.com/food-history:origin-of-the-word-candy/.

Tucker, Aimee. January 1, 2019. "New England Made, Necco Wafers: The History (and Sad Demise) of America's Oldest Candy," *New England Today: Food.* https://newengland.com/today/food/new-england-made/necco-wafers/.

CHAPTER 3

IT'S ABOUT TIME

INTRODUCTION

The concept of time may refer to an event in history such as the moonwalk or Woodstock, or it may refer to traditional events that are celebrated throughout the year such as birthdays or Valentine's Day. It may also refer to a particular time of the day or an appointment or meeting. In this chapter, many aspects of time are covered.

Each of the programs in this chapter is presented as an outline that includes a description of the program, beginning discussion questions, supplies needed, program instructions along with additional activities that could be included, and suggestions for working with older adults attending the program. Annual events and traditions such as baseball, Thanksgiving, and Valentine's Day are included. Other programs outline events and trends that were popular during the growing-up years of different generations, such as music or popular TV shows. Older adults may also enjoy games or quizzes about events during their lifetime, such as a trivia game about a popular television show.

BASEBALL: AMERICA'S FAVORITE PASTIME

Program by Phyllis Goodman

Description

Baseball is one of America's favorite pastimes. Many people have a favorite hometown or national team they support. It is a fun topic to discuss especially in the spring when the baseball season begins. This program discusses baseball, in general, and includes the traditions, trivia, and stories about baseball. This program can also be modified to talk about local or a favorite baseball team.

Supplies/Materials Needed

- Baseball props—baseball glove, baseball, box of Cracker Jacks, baseball bat, and so on
- Laminated pictures or PowerPoint of baseball traditions—things like a baseball glove, the seventh-inning stretch, baseball game food, and so on
- Lyrics to "Take Me Out to the Ball Game" by Jack Norworth
- "Casey at the Bat" by Ernest Lawrence Thayer
- CD of Abbott and Costello's "Who's On First"
- Famous Baseball Players Trivia Quiz (taken from ElderSong Publications, Inc., activity newsletter, 2014)

Program Instructions

1. Arrive early to set up the room so that everyone can see and hear. Greet participants as they come into the room or finish up a previous activity.

2. Seat the residents in a semicircle or around a table so they can see you and one another.

3. Introduce the theme to the group, and begin the discussion with questions about their favorite baseball teams and memories about going to a baseball game:

   a. Which is your favorite baseball team?

   b. How old were you when you went to your first baseball game? What do you remember about it?

   c. Did you play baseball as a child? What was the name of your team?

   d. Did you collect baseball cards?

   e. What are your favorite baseball traditions/memories?

4. Pass around the props and ask participants to talk about a special memory or tradition that they associate with the prop.

5. The chorus to the song "Take Me Out to the Ball Game" by Jack Norworth is a baseball tradition. To get things started for the next activity, sing "Take Me Out to the Ball Game." Place the lyrics to the song on the computer or in large font on poster board (Library of Congress, 2019b).

6. Talk about baseball traditions, giving a few facts about each one. Use pictures printed on cardstock and laminated, pictures on a computer, or books from the library collection with large, clear pictures. Some of the traditions might include the history of the "Take Me Out to the Ball Game" song, the seventh-inning stretch, singing the National Anthem, eating Cracker Jacks and hot dogs at a game, the

first pitch by a president, singing "Sweet Caroline" at Fenway Park, and bringing a baseball glove to the game (information for this activity was taken from these resources: Library of Congress, 2019a; Turner Broadcasting System, 2019; Casano, 2019; Vecsey, 2006).

a. **"Take Me Out to the Ball Game"**: The lyrics of the song were written by songwriter Jack Norworth in 1908, and music was added by Albert Von Tilzer. The first time it was sung at a ballpark is believed to be in 1934. Two verses of the song are about Katie Casey, who asked her boyfriend to go to a baseball game instead of a show. "Take Me Out to the Ball Game" is actually the chorus to the song. By the 1950s it was baseball's anthem for the seventh-inning stretch. It appeared in movies such as *A Night at the Opera*, *The Naughty Nineties*, and *Take Me out to the Ball Game.*

b. **"Casey at the Bat"**: If sports had its own poem, "Casey at the Bat" by Ernest Lawrence Thayer would belong to baseball. The poem was written in 1888 about a hometown batter who had a chance to make fans happy.

c. **Seventh-inning stretch:** The origin of this, though most likely a legend, is that during a 1910 game, President William Taft got up to stretch in the middle of the seventh inning, and out of respect, the crowd joined him as well. Thus, at the top of the seventh inning, fans stretch a bit, walk around, get a snack, and drink.

d. **The national anthem:** Baseball was the first sport to have the national anthem sung before the beginning of the game. To support the military and to show patriotism, the national anthem has been sung for every game since World War II. The anthem was even performed once in a while during the nineteenth century.

e. **Cracker Jacks and other baseball game food:** This snack was introduced at the 1893 Chicago World's Fair by a local popcorn company and was first sold at some ballparks in 1907. Once the product was linked to the "Take Me Out to the Ball Game" song, sales of the snack rose. In addition to Cracker Jacks, nachos, soda, and hotdogs are all enjoyed at baseball games.

f. **First pitch:** This tradition began in 1910 when President William Taft threw out the first pitch at the Washington Senators game. Since then, the incumbent president usually throws out the first pitch at a big game.

g. **Keeping a baseball hit into the stands by a player:** In the early 1900s fans were expected to return baseballs that they caught during the game. If a fan tried to keep the ball, ushers confronted the person, resulting often in frequent fights and arrests. The owner of the Cubs, growing tired of the incidents, allowed fans to keep a ball they caught. The idea did not catch on until the 1930s when a fan who caught a ball sued the team after being beaten by ushers.

h. **Taking a baseball glove to the game:** Fans will often bring their own glove to a baseball game just in case they are sitting where a foul ball ends up.

i. **"Sweet Caroline" at Fenway Park:** The song "Sweet Caroline" began to be played in the middle of the eighth inning in 2002 at Fenway Park and has caught on. This is a favorite for Boston Red Sox and Fenway Park fans.

j. **Fireworks:** Many ballparks have their own special traditions. At a Reds game in Cincinnati, Ohio, fireworks are shot off after a home run. For other leagues they are part of the postgame events.

7. Read the poem "Casey at the Bat" by Ernest Lawrence Thayer.

8. Listen to the audio CD of Abbott and Costello's "Who's On First."

9. Play the famous Baseball Players Trivia Quiz (from ElderSong Publications, Inc., 2014; activity newsletter).

Famous Baseball Players Trivia Quiz

a. Who was the first African American to play major league baseball in 1947, signing with the Brooklyn Dodgers? **Jackie Robinson**

b. What team did power hitter Mickey Mantle play for? **New York Yankees**

c. Which New York Yankees slugger was nicknamed the "Sultan of Swat"? **Babe Ruth**

d. Which Hall of Fame pitcher for the St. Louis Cardinals had a brother named Daffy? **Dizzy Dean**

e. What was the nickname of NY Yankees star Lou Gehrig, who played in over 2,100 consecutive games? **Iron Horse**

f. What was the nickname for Yankee centerfielder Joe DiMaggio? **Joltin' Joe**

g. The "Say Hey Kid" was baseball's National League Rookie of the Year in 1951, and later became a superstar for the New York/San Francisco Giants. Who was he? **Willie Mays**

h. Which New York Yankee Hall of Fame catcher played in the World Series 14 times and was known for his humorous one-liners? **Yogi Berra**

i. What do the following baseball players have in common: CY Young, Lefty Grove, Walter Johnson, Sandy Koufax, Bob Gibson, Tom Seaver, and Nolan Ryan? **All were great pitchers**.

j. What position did Cal Ripken Jr. of the Baltimore Orioles play? **Shortstop**

This quiz originally appeared in Baseball's Fall Classic Newsletter, September 1, 2014. Copyright ElderSong Publications, Inc. Used by permission.

Suggestions/Tips for Interacting with Residents

- When using pictures make sure the font/picture is large enough to be seen by everyone.
- Offer magnifiers for those with vision problems, or explain what is going on in the photo.
- Ask questions throughout the program to keep the discussion going.

Program Variations

- Baseball Americana is a PowerPoint presentation that is available on the Library of Congress website, https://www.loc.gov/exhibitions/baseball-americana/about-this-exhibition/. The Library of Congress and the Baseball Hall of Fame websites have several baseball presentations and photos as well.
- Bring a collection of books from the library's collections with clear, large pictures of famous baseball players to pass around. Briefly talk about the players as their pictures are being passed around.
- Book talk fiction books about baseball. These are a few suggestions, but check your library's collection for other titles.

   a. *Three Strikes and You're Dead* by Jessica Fletcher and Donald Bain

   b. *The Girl Who Loved Tom Gordon* by Stephen King

   c. *Foul Play* by Tori Carrington

   d. *Shoeless Joe* by W. P. Kinsella

   e. *Calico Joe* by John Grisham

   f. *The Great American Novel* by Philip Roth

• Show a trailer or clip from a baseball movie.

REFERENCES

Casano, Ann. 2018. "The Best Team and Ballpark Traditions in MLB." https://www.ranker.com/list/baseball-stadium-team-traditions/anncasano?page=6 (check this site for some unique ballpark traditions).

ElderSong Publications, Inc. September 1, 2014. "Famous Baseball Players Trivia Quiz." https://blog.eldersong.com/2014/09/baseballs-fall-classic/.

Library of Congress. 2019a. "Baseball Americana." https://www.loc.gov/exhibitions/baseball-americana/about-this-exhibition/.

Library of Congress. 2019b. "Take Me Out to the Ball Game." www.loc.gov/item/ihas.200153239.

Turner Broadcasting System. 2019. https://bleacherreport.com/articles/538149-50-best-traditions-in-baseball#slide27.

Vecsey, George. 2006. *Baseball: A History of America's Favorite Game.* New York: Modern Library.

LOCAL HISTORY PROGRAMS

Program by Phyllis Goodman

Description

Local history provides many opportunities for programs. These types of programs provide an opportunity to explore community historical events and connections. It allows participants an opportunity to reminisce about events they may have been involved in or to share stories they heard from parents and grandparents. These type of programs can be presented in a variety of ways, including a slide show with narration, partnering with the local historical society, or combining trivia games and quizzes with a slide show.

Supplies/Materials Needed

- Flash drive with the slide show.
- Computer to connect to a large screen monitor.
- If a monitor is not available, use a projector and screen or blank wall.
- Books with large pictures that relate to the theme.
- Trivia games, quizzes of fill-in-the-blank activities.

Program Instructions

1. Arrive early to set up the computer and other equipment. Greet participants as they enter the room or finish up a previous activity.
2. Seat participants in a semicircle or around a table so they can see each other, the slide show and other materials. Prepare the slides so that the photos are large and clear enough to see. Use a large font for text on the slide, and keep the information brief. Speak in a clear voice, and check once in a while that the audience can hear you.
3. If your program is around lunch time, ask the activity coordinator if a lunch that relates to the theme could be served that day. For instance, before a program about the Cincinnati Reds baseball team, the facility served Skyline Chili for lunch to kick off the program.
4. Ask questions during the slide show to encourage discussion.

Subjects for Local History Programs

- If you do not know much about the history of your community, talk with the local history society or browse the local history section of your library. The local history society may be willing to partner with you to present the program.
- Architecture—early buildings, music halls, theaters, and so on.
- Historical events that had an impact on the community such as Morgan's Raid, the Underground Railroad, or Prohibition, a major flood, or other weather events that impacted the area.
- Amusement parks or local entertainment venues.
- Famous residents—Rosemary Clooney, Frank Sinatra, Ronald Reagan, Doris Day, Will Rogers, Bonnie and Clyde.
- Local orchestra or symphony.
- Local radio stations or shows.

Suggestions/Tips for Interacting with Residents

- When using audiovisual equipment such as slide shows or audio recordings, arrive early so that you can set up the equipment so that everyone will be able to see and hear.
- When creating a slide show, make sure the pictures are clear and large enough to see. Add a small amount of text, so those in the audience with hearing loss will be able to read the information and follow along.
- Encourage participants to bring up questions and information during the presentation.

CINCINNATI: THEN AND NOW

Program by Phyllis Goodman

Description

This is an example of a local history program about changes in Cincinnati over a hundred years called Cincinnati—Then and Now. The program took place after lunch, so the center provided Cincinnati Chili and hot dogs for lunch. Afterward we talked about how Cincinnati had changed over the years using games, music, and historical information. This was a fun program especially for one of my groups who enjoyed local history and was always eager to talk about their experiences.

Supplies/Materials Needed

- PowerPoint slide show with Cincinnati landmarks and points of interest today and a hundred years ago
- Erich Kunzel and the Cincinnati Pops (information taken from the website https://www.cincinnatisymphony.org/your-visit/music-hall/history/ and music CD)
- Cincinnati Jeopardy game
- Cincinnati Stories

  Vignettes: Intriguing Short Stories of Interest about the Queen City, Cincinnati by Charles Bruce Duncan, 1972

  Stories in the Grove by Phillip J. Nuxhall, Orange Frazer Press, 2014

Program Instructions

1. Arrive early to set up the equipment and to organize your information. Greet participants as they enter the room or finish up a previous activity.
2. Seat participants in a semicircle or around a table so they can see the slide show and jeopardy board. Prepare the slides so that the photos are large and clear enough to see. Use a large font for text on the slide, and keep the information brief. Speak in a clear voice, and check once in a while that the audience can hear you.
3. Introduce the theme, and start the discussion with questions about the participants' experiences in Cincinnati:
   a. Did you grow up in Cincinnati? Which neighborhood?
   b. What do you remember about your neighborhood?
   c. Did you go shopping downtown at McAlpins, Lazarus, or Shillito Rikes department stores?
   d. Did you ever go to a Cincinnati Pops concert?
4. Play music performed by the Cincinnati Pops, and share some facts about the Pops orchestra (information taken from the Cincinnati Symphony orchestra's website https://www.cincinnatisymphony.org/your-visit/music-hall/history/) for this part.
   a. Erich Kunzel was the conductor of the Cincinnati Pops from 1977 through 2009. Before that he was the conductor of the Cincinnati Symphony Orchestra.
   b. The Pops members also play in the Cincinnati Symphony Orchestra.
   c. The Cincinnati Pops won a Grammy Award for the Pops' *Copland: Music of America* in 1998.
   d. John Morris Russell became the director of the Cincinnati Pops and Symphony orchestras in 2009 after Erich Kunzel's death.

5. Show pictures or a slide show, prepared in advance, of landmarks in Cincinnati from one hundred years ago and currently. Ask what the landmark or location is and what they remember about it. Share an interesting fact or two about each place (information for this activity was taken from the following resources: Giglierano, 1988; Grace and White, 2002; Kock, 2003).

   a. Fountain Square—Officially known as the Tyler Davidson Fountain, it was dedicated in Cincinnati in 1871. Its original location was on a wide esplanade in the middle of Fifth Street. Later, it was redesigned and moved south of the plaza.

   b. Music Hall—Built in 1878, it is the home of the Cincinnati Symphony and Pops orchestra, the opera, and the Cincinnati Ballet. It became a national historic landmark in 1975 and served as the city's first convention center. It has hosted many entertainers, including Frank Sinatra, Elton John, Janis Joplin, and Eric Clapton.

   c. Sawyer Point—It was once a hub for steamboat traffic and warehouses along Cincinnati's riverfront. Today it makes up a mile-long stretch of parkland with a performance pavilion and tennis and volleyball courts.

   d. Mt. Adam incline—At one time, Cincinnati had five inclines. The Mt. Adam incline was the most popular incline transporting people from downtown to Eden Park. At the top of the incline was a resort and park. It opened in 1876 and closed in 1948.

   e. Cincinnati Union Terminal—The Union Terminal began construction in 1929 and was completed in 1933. When it opened, it had a vibrant railroad hub designed to accommodate 17,000 passengers and 216 trains a day. Today, it is called the Cincinnati Museum Center and houses the Cincinnati History Museum, Museum of Natural History & Science, and the Children's Museum.

   f. Findlay Market—Cincinnati was once home to nine public markets in the nineteenth and early twentieth centuries. Findlay Market, built in 1852, was one of the first buildings using iron frame construction technology and one of the few to survive. It has been renovated several times and remains a vibrant market especially during the summer months.

   g. Cincinnati Zoo Elephant House—The Cincinnati Zoo is one of the top zoos in the country and is especially known for its Elephant House, which was built in 1906. When it opened, it was known as the Herbivora House, which housed a variety of creatures like kangaroos, rhinos, hippos, bison, and elephants. The building has undergone several renovations and now, known as the Elephant Reserve, is home to giraffes, okapis, and elephants.

6. Cincinnati Jeopardy game.

   a. This version of Jeopardy can be played in a variety of ways. For this program a science board was used. The name of a category was written on large envelopes and attached to the science board. The prepared index cards were placed in the envelopes.

   b. The categories used are Transportation, History, Entertainment, Education and Art, Shopping, and Businesses. Each category was represented by a different color index card, with white index cards used for a tiebreaker. On each card a question about a particular category was written along with its answer.

   c. The game begins by asking one of the participants to pick a category. Pull a card from the category envelope, read the statement, and ask participants to raise their hands if they know the answer. The person who knows the correct answer is given the card.

   d. Ask the participants if they have any special memories or connections to the question asked.

   e. Once all the questions are answered, everyone counts the number of cards they have. The person with the most cards wins the game. In case of a tie, the tiebreaker questions are asked.

   f. Optional: Award a small prize to the winner (a postcard of Cincinnati or library swag or donated books).

Questions Used from the Cincinnati Jeopardy Game

Businesses

i.   This company is located on Spring Grove Avenue and began as a retail meat market. In the 1980s it was the largest meat processing firm. The American Beauty Rose is its trademark. **Kahn's & Company**

ii. This company was started in 1862 with a $2,000 investment. In 1889, the company manufactured reed organs and built its first piano in 1891. **Baldwin Piano Company**

iii. By the mid-1950s, this was one of the largest breweries in Ohio. It survived Prohibition by manufacturing soft drinks and "near beer." **Hudepohl Brewing Company**

iv. Organized in 1846, this company produced cotton wadding and later made mattresses. **Stearns & Foster**

v.   Now closed, this company was originally known as the Cincinnati Screw & Tap Company. It was located in Oakley and was a leader in robotics and machinery for the plastics industry. **Cincinnati Milling Machine, Milacron**

Education and Art

i.   Built in 1878 with private money, it is the home to the Cincinnati Pops and Symphony orchestras, the Opera, and the Ballet. It was used as the city's first convention center. **Music Hall**

ii. This is one of Cincinnati's oldest high schools and is located on Madison Road. It was named after a Cincinnati physician and surgeon who enforced an anti-spitting ordinance. **Withrow High School**

iii. This school opened in 1953 as Central Vocational High School. It is located on Central Parkway and now has a new name. **Cincinnati State Technical and Community College**

iv. This building was known as the "Windings" and was built around 1868. It was the home of William Clifford Neff and later became the home of an all-girls boarding school located in Clifton. What is the name of the school? **Academy of the Sacred Heart**

v.   This pottery was first fired in 1880 in a building on Eastern Avenue. It gained a worldwide reputation as distinctive artwork and moved its site to Mt. Adams in 1892 and then to Mississippi in 1960. Production stopped in 1967. **Rookwood Pottery**

Entertainment and Amusement

i.   This was a favorite nightspot located in Southgate, Kentucky. In May 1977 it was destroyed by fire. **Beverly Hills Supper Club**

ii. This amusement park was located on Spring Grove Avenue. In the early 1900s it had a swimming lake, opera house, dance hall, Hilarity Hall, Blue Streak Roller Coaster, and the Derby Racer. It closed due to failure to pay its water bill. **Chester Park**

iii. One of Cincinnati's largest sports arena until Riverfront Coliseum was built. It hosted the Cincinnati Royals pro basketball, concerts, and the Ice Capades. **Cincinnati Gardens**

iv. This German eatery opened in Over-the-Rhine in 1872 as a saloon. Later, it was turned into a German restaurant. In 1984, Jim Tarbell purchased it and attempted to preserve it as a historic institution. **Grammer's Restaurant**

v.   A well-known Cincinnati amusement park before Kings Island. It is known for such rides as Lost River, Wildcat, Laugh in the Dark, Teddy Bear, and Shooting Star. **Coney Island**

History

i. This suburb located in northwestern Springfield Township was created by the federal government in the 1930s as an experiment in community planning and design and to solve some of the problems brought on by the Depression. It boasts a "green belt." **Greenhills**

ii. This market house opened in 1855 and is the only surviving public market places. Its merchants and business owners sponsor the Reds Opening Day Parade. **Findlay Market**

iii. In 1884 this gentleman led the presidential campaign for James Blaine. Though Blaine lost the election, this person became the "boss" of Cincinnati politics. In order to get a job in politics, one had to get his approval. **George B. Cox**

iv. This statue and fountain was placed in the middle of Fifth Street in 1871 and portrayed the uses of water. The statue was given to the city by Harry Probasco in honor of this deceased business partner and brother-in-law. **Tyler Davidson Fountain**

v. This town was the home of President William Harrison. It was founded by John Cleves Symmes in 1789 in hopes that it would become the metropolis of the Ohio Valley. **North Bend, Ohio**

Shopping

i. Name the dry goods store located on Central Parkway between Sycamore and Main. Serving primarily residents living in Over-the-Rhine, it closed in April 1954 due to poor sales. It is currently used for the Hamilton County Jobs and Family Services offices. **Alms & Doepke**

ii. Due to a late train, two Detroit merchants opened this store at Fifth & Vine on March 26, 1877. In 1978 it was bought by the Elder-Beerman stores. **Mabley & Carew**

iii. This store has had several names and locations. It had locations on Fourth Street, a six-story location at Seventh and Race streets and at Fifth and Vine streets. **Shillito, Shillito-Rikes, Lazarus, and Macy's**

iv. Founded by brothers Henry and Samuel in 1863, this dry goods store was a fixture at Fourth and Race Streets. They merged with L. S. Ayres, and the building was demolished in 1988 to build the Tower Place Mall. **H&S Pogue**

v. This store founder joined B. A. Branagan to establish the Great Western Tea Company at 66 Pearle Street when his family finances were destroyed in the 1883 panic. He later bought out his partner and changed the name of the stores to his last name. The parent company is still located in downtown Cincinnati. **Kroger Stores (Bernard H. Kroger)**

Transportation

i. Once owned by the Greene Line Steamer, Inc., Capt. Tome Greene bought this steam boat in California. It was brought to Cincinnati by way of the Panama Canal. Annually this steamboat raced on the Ohio River with the Belle of Louisville. **Delta Queen**

ii. This canal followed the path that is now Central Parkway. In the early twentieth century it became obsolete as the automobile replaced it as a means of transportation. **Miami & Erie Canal**

iii. Originally, this was built for railroad traffic. It is one of the world's grandest Art Deco Structures and currently houses the Cincinnati History Museum, Museum of Natural History & Science, and the Children's Museum. **Union Terminal, Cincinnati Museum Center**

iv. This viaduct opened in 1914 and linked the Northside and Cannonsville to Cincinnati and was used by both streetcars and automobiles. **Ludlow Avenue Viaduct**

v. Cincinnati is also known as the city with seven hills. Early in its history inclines were built around the city to aid transportation up and down some of the hills. Name an incline and tell something about it. **Mt. Adams, Mt. Auburn, Elm St., Price Hill, and Fairview**

Tiebreaker Questions

i. This animal jumped a six-foot fence at the Ken Meyer meat company in Mt. Washington in 2002. For eleven days she eluded police and the public by hiding out in the brush at Mount Storm Park in Clifton. **Cow (Cinci Freedom)**

ii. This person became a catcher for the Cincinnati Reds in 1968 when he was named the National League Rookie of the Year. **Johnny Bench**

Information for questions used in this activity was taken from Ford (1987), Green (1986), Kock (2003), Painter (2006), Seuss (2016), and Singer (2004).

---

7. Cincinnati stories. Share some vignettes about Cincinnati or interesting stories about those who are buried in Spring Grove Cemetery from Phillip Nuxhall's book, *Stories in the Grove.*

Suggestions/Tips for Interacting with Residents

• Bring a preapproved snack, or ask the center to make a special lunch or snack to go along with the theme of the program.

• During the jeopardy games, face the audience and make eye contact while reading the questions.

Program Variations

• An alternative to the jeopardy board is to write the categories on a white board or poster board in large font. Read questions that relate to each category. Have the participants keep score on a score sheet.

• Create a Cincinnati Quiz, and see how many questions the group can answer correctly.

• Bring in a collection of books about Cincinnati that have large, clear pictures. Pass the book around with the item/landmark you are talking about for the participants to look at. Ask questions and encourage participants to share stories or things they remember about the location or landmark.

REFERENCES

Cincinnati Symphony Orchestra. 2019. "Our History." https://www.cincinnatisymphony.org/your-visit/music-hall/history/.

Ford, Kate B. 1987. *History of Cincinnati, Ohio with Illustrations and Biographical Sketches.* Cincinnati: Ohio Bookstore.

Giglierano, Geoffrey. 1988. *The Bicentennial Guide to Greater Cincinnati: A Portrait of Two Hundred Years.* Cincinnati: Cincinnati Historical Society.

Grace, Kevin, and Tom White. 2002. *Cincinnati Revealed: A Photographic Heritage of the Queen City.* Charleston, SC: Arcadia Publishing.

Green, Marilyn. 1986. *Cincinnati, a Pictorial History.* Brookfield, MO: Donning Publishing Co.

Kock, Barbara. 2003. *Cincinnati: A Reflection of Her Present and Her Past.* Cincinnati: Price Hill Historical Society.

Painter, Sue. 2006. *Architecture in Cincinnati: An Illustrated History of Designing and Building an American City.* Cincinnati: Ohio University Press.

Seuss, Jeff. 2016. *Hidden History of Cincinnati.* Charleston, SC: History Press.

Singer, Allen J. 2004. *Cincinnati on the Go: History of Mass Transit.* Charleston, SC: Arcadia Publishing.

MUSIC OF THE DECADES

Program by Phyllis Goodman

Description

Music is found in every culture and generation. While there are crossovers of musical favorites between generations, every generation or culture has a style of music that defines its youth. Many programs for older adults are presented to an audience that is made up of individuals from different generations and have different interests. This program was designed to cover music and artists from the 1940s to the 1960s and includes a variety of activities. This program could also be done by focusing on one musical era, famous musical artists, or genre of music.

Supplies/Materials Needed

- PowerPoint slide show of artists and music from the three decades—1940s, 1950s, and 1960s.
- Video of "Twenty Five Dances through the Decades" on YouTube.

Program Instructions

1. Arrive early to set up the equipment and to organize your materials for the program. Greet participants as they enter the room or finish a previous activity.

2. Seat participants in a semicircle or around a table so they can see the slide show or other material that is being shown. Prepare the slides so that the photos are large and clear enough to see. Use a large font for text on the slide, and keep the information brief. Speak in a clear voice, and check once in a while that the audience can hear you.

3. Introduce the theme of the program, and begin the discussion with questions about the music the audience listened to as young adults such as the following:

   a. Which musicians did you listen to when you were growing up? Why did you like their music?

   b. What did your parents or older adults think about your music?

   c. How did you listen to music—with a record player, a transistor radio, a cassette player?

   d. Did you ever go to a live concert? Where? Who performed/what kind of music was it?

   e. Did you enjoy dancing to your favorite music? What dances do you remember doing?

   f. Did you buy music albums? Did you purchase music albums with your own money?

4. Create a PowerPoint slide show prior to the program with the music and pictures of top musical artists from the 1940s, 1950s and 1960s. Using the PowerPoint program link a song of the artist to their picture on the slide.

5. While showing the picture of the artist, play one of their songs. Ask participants what the name of the song is. Share a few facts about the artist with the group (information for this activity was taken from Gorlinski, 2010; Leight, 2014; Motown Museum, 2016; Rolling Stone, 2010; Top 40 Weekly, 2016a, 2016b).

General Information

Music of the 1940s consisted of big band music and jazz with popular artists like Ella Fitzgerald, Benny Goodman, Frank Sinatra, Bing Crosby, and Perry Como. With many Americans fighting in World War II, many songs centered on the home front and the war.

Music of the 1950s saw the birth of rock and roll with artists such as Bill Haley and Elvis Presley. It reflected the innocence and optimism of the young people growing up in the 1950s who hadn't experienced the war. Folk music from artists such as Pat Boone, Perry Como, and Patti Page coexisted alongside the rock and roll music of the day.

Music of the 1960s began with a continuation of the rock and roll sounds of the 1950s. TV shows such as *American Bandstand* helped to promote new songs and dance styles such as the Twist, the Locomotion, and the Mashed Potato. The British invasion changed the musical styles with the music of the Beatles, Herman's Hermits, Donovan, Petula Clark, the Animals, and the Rolling Stones. During the second half of the 1960s, music began to reflect the social unrest, Vietnam War, and discontent of the era.

Popular Music Artists from the 1940s, 1950s, and 1960s

- **Ella Fitzgerald**—Ella Fitzgerald was known for her wide vocal range and smoothness of her voice. Her career as a singer spanned for more than six decades, and she toured with pop and jazz stars such as Benny Goodman, Louis Armstrong, and Duke Ellington. She was one of the best-selling jazz vocal artists in the 1940s and for years was the main attraction at Norman Ganz's Philharmonic concerts.

  Songs—"Love and Kisses," "It Don't Mean a Thing (If It Ain't Got That Swing)"

- **Duke Ellington**—Duke Ellington began playing the piano at an early age and became an influential jazz composer in the 1930s and 1940s. He led his band for over fifty years, which included noted musicians Cootie Williams, Rex Stewart, and Lawrence Brown with their unique sound.

  Songs—"Take the 'A' Train," "In a Sentimental Mood"

- **Nat King Cole**—Nat King Cole was considered one of the influential pianists of the swing era. It was his unique singing voice and style, however, that brought him success. Cole formed the King Cole Trio in the 1930s, which experienced much success with several jazz recordings. He eventually left the Trio behind for mainstream pop. Cole performed on his own TV show (*The Nat King Cole Show* in 1956), on stage, and in the movies, remaining popular until his death.

  Songs—"Straighten Up and Fly Right," "Unforgettable"

- **Frank Sinatra**—Frank Sinatra began his entertainment career as a singer with a local singing group. Later joining the Dorsey band and Columbia records, Sinatra recorded such songs as "I'll Never Smile Again" and "Put Your Dreams Away." By the late 1940s Sinatra was considered a has-been due to bad press about his involvement with the mafia, loss of Columbia's record contracts, and the cancelation of his show. He began acting in movies in the 1950s and went on to become one of the top film stars.

  Songs—"My Way," "I've Got You under My Skin." *Movies*—*Manchurian Candidate*, *From Here to Eternity*

- **Patsy Cline**—Patsy Cline, country and western singer, helped close the gap between country and mainstream music. She began her career by singing with local bands and gained a wider audience with the emergence of television in the late 1950s. After winning a prize on the *Arthur Godfrey's Talent Scouts* television show, she gained national exposure and became a regular on the *Grand Ole Opry* radio broadcasts in Nashville. She died in an airplane crash in 1963 at the age of 31.

  Songs—"Walkin after Midnight," "I Fall to Pieces"

- **Elvis Presley**—Singer, songwriter, and actor, Presley is referred to as the "king of rock and roll." Presley combined country and rhythm and blues (R&B) music and is considered to have a major influence on future rock stars John Lennon, Bruce Springsteen, and Bob Dylan. Growing up in Memphis, Elvis Presley had many opportunities to hear R&B, gospel, country, and mainstream popular music. With the release of "Heartbreak Hotel" in 1956 he moved away from country and into a new era of music with his dress, moves, tenor voice, and "rockability." At the end of his career, he suffered medical problems from prescription drug abuse.

Songs—"Jailhouse Rock," "Heartbreak Hotel"

- **Chuck Berry**—Singer, guitarist, and songwriter, Chuck Berry performed rhythm and blues and rock and roll from the 1950s to the 1970s. In 1955 he signed with the Chess Label recording studio and produced "Maybellene," which stayed on the pop charts for eleven weeks. His descriptions of the teen culture with short sentences and distinct stories made him popular with both white and black teens. Known for his distinct sounds and combining the R&B sound with country music, he is considered one of the most influential artists in the history of rock and roll. His music has been recorded by many music performers, and his song "Johnny B. Goode" was one of the songs placed on a copper phonograph record put on the side of the *Voyager 1* satellite.

Songs—"Maybellene," "Roll Over Beethoven"

- **Ray Charles**—Pianist, singer, songwriter, and bandleader, Ray Charles is credited with the early creation of soul music, a style that combined gospel, R&B, and jazz. His music career began at age five on a piano in a nearby café until his blindness took him to a school for the deaf and blind. At age fifteen he left school to play professionally. His arrangement for "The Things That I Used to Do" for Guitar Slim became a blues million-dollar seller in 1953. He formed his own recording labels and was inducted into the Rock and Roll Hall of Fame in 1986.

Songs—"Georgia on My Mind," "Hit the Road, Jack"

- **Buddy Holly and the Crickets**—The African American rhythm and blues playing on the radio had a big impact on Holly and other white teens who listened to it in the 1950s. Buddy Holly, who was already a performer in the musical styles of country, bluegrass, and gospel, was devoted to R&B. However, in 1955 after hearing Elvis Presley, he switched to rock and roll. Holly formed the group Buddy Holly and the Crickets, which produced a unique sound by experimenting with unique techniques, like placing the microphone in different places, echo chamber effects, and overdubbing (superimposing one recording onto another). In 1959, estranged from the Crickets and in need of money he participated in the "Winter Dance Party of 1959" tour with Ritchie Valens and the Big Bopper. All three were killed in a plane crash. Their songs, which they wrote mostly themselves; their studio techniques; and their music had a major influence on the Beatles.

Songs—"Peggy Sue," "That'll Be the Day"

- **Motown Artists**—Marvin Gaye, Smokey Robinson and the Miracles, Four Tops, Gladys Knight and the Pips, Stevie Wonder, Martha and the Vandellas, Temptations, and the Supremes are just a few of the groups that came out of Motown, in Detroit, Michigan. Motown was founded by Berry Gordy as a musical studio, which was the first African American–owned record company turning out many successful musical groups. The Motown artists combined the sounds of black gospel music with the bebop jazz sound.

Songs—"What's Going On" (Marvin Gaye), "You've Really Got a Hold on Me" (Smokey Robinson), "My Girl" (Temptations), "Baby Love" (Supremes)

- **Bob Dylan**—Bob Dylan began his music career by playing folk music with his harmonica and guitar in coffeehouses. His songs were influenced by the work of Woody Guthrie and poets like Allen Ginsberg. His wide repertoire included performing songs of a personal nature to protest songs. In 2009 he was awarded the Pulitzer Prize "for his profound impact on popular music and American culture."

Songs—"Blowin in the Wind," "Like a Rolling Stone"

- **The Beatles**—The Beatles were formed by self-taught musicians, John Lennon and Paul McCartney, who played together in Liverpool in 1957. They were later joined by George Harrison. Their name was inspired by Buddy Holly and the Crickets, and they rose to fame with original tunes and classic

American rock and roll. In 1964, Beatlemania crossed the ocean with the appearance of the Beatles on American TV. Over the years the Beatles experimented and widely increased their music repertoire from pop songs like "Yesterday" to hard rock with songs like "Norwegian Wood." In 1970 the group broke up due to disagreements and accusations. All four members of the group went on to produce their own albums. John Lennon created a new sound with his wife Yoko Ono, and Paul McCartney formed the band Wings.

Songs—"Yesterday," "Hey Jude," "I Want to Hold Your Hand"

- **The Rolling Stones**—The original members of the Rolling Stones were Mick Jagger, Keith Richards, Brian Jones, Bill Wyman, and Charlie Watts. This British rock group was formed in 1962, and by 1965 their popularity was second to the Beatles. While the Beatles were more polished, the Stones had longer hair, wore different clothes, and appeared intimidating. Their music style was based on Chicago blues, with a darker quality to it. Early on they played the blues and rock and roll music of 1950s' artists. In the 1960s they began writing and playing their own music, which was often about subjects that were considered taboo: drugs, sex, and violence.

  Songs—"I Can't Get No Satisfaction," "Paint It Black"

- **The Beach Boys**—The original members of the Beach Boys were Brian Wilson, Dennis Wilson, Carl Wilson, Michael Love, and Alan Jardine. Encouraged to pursue music, the group wrote songs about the beach and surfing. The success of "Surfin" in 1962 led a contract with Capitol records. Brian Wilson continued to write almost all of the groups songs, with many appearing on Billboard's U.S. singles charts. In 1963 Brian took over complete artistic control.

  Songs—"Surfin," "I Get Around"

- **Aretha Franklin**—Aretha Franklin grew up in Detroit and joined her father on his gospel programs as he toured throughout the country. Franklin switched to secular music at eighteen and signed a contract with Columbia in New York City. Struggling to cross over to mainstream music, she switched to Atlantic Records where she created her own musical style. Labeled the "queen of soul," her music often reflected the culture of the day. In 1987 she was inducted into the Rock and Roll Hall of Fame and was the first woman to receive that honor.

  Songs—"Respect," "Think"

- **Jimi Hendrix**—Singer, songwriter, and guitarist, Hendrix combined the blues, jazz, rock, and soul to define the electric guitar in his own way. His career lasted for four years and was known for playing at high volume. His music repertoire ranged from hard rock to ballads.

  Songs—"Purple Haze," "Hey Joe"

- **Little Richard**—Before Elvis, Little Richard in 1951 was recording for RCA-Victor (Camden) records. The rock and roll music of his time was called "African Music" or "voodoo music," but it was very popular among white teens.

  Songs—"Good Golly Miss Molly," "Tutti Frutti"

- **The Shirelles**—Shirley Alston Reeves provided the group's lead vocals with a sentimental sound. They weren't the first girl group, but they had many hits. They influenced many other groups such as the Ronettes, Motown's Supremes, and the Beatles.

  Songs—"Baby It's You," "Will You Love Me Tomorrow"

- **The Who**—The Who was known for creating the rock opera in the 1960s and 1970s. Though more popular in the United Kingdom than in the United States, The Who sang about teenage angst, alienation, frustration, and uncertainty. Most of their concerts ended with Pete Townshend smashing his guitar. Their performance of "Tommy" at Woodstock in 1969 made them stars on the rock and roll stage.

  Songs—"Tommy," "Won't Get Fooled Again"

- **Janis Joplin**—American singer and songwriter of rock, soul, and blues, Janis Joplin was known for her high, husky, and earthy voice. She was influenced by the music of Bessie Smith and Big Mama Thornton and was drawn to the Haight Ashbury neighborhood in San Francisco. Her musical range and wails gave her the label "greatest white urban blues and soul singer of her generation." Joplin died from a heroin overdose in 1970. She was inducted into the Rock and Roll Hall of Fame in 1995.

    Songs—"Me and Bobby McGee," "Piece of My Heart"

6. Music isn't complete unless one can dance to it. Over the decades many dances have become as popular as the music itself. Play the YouTube video "Twenty Five Dances through the Decades," https://www.youtube.com/watch?v=rUeWdFJBglo. Encourage participants to participate using hand movements or their feet while still sitting. After the video talk to participants about their dance experiences.

Suggestions/Tips for Interacting with Residents

- Encourage participants to participate in the dance movements if they can. If they do not wish to participate, encourage them to stay and listen.
- Ask questions throughout the program to encourage discussion.
- Be sure everyone can hear the music being played.

Program Variations

- Show the video "Nine Dance Crazes through the Decades," http://www.everythingzoomer.com/lifestyle/spirit/nostalgia/2015/08/29/9-dance-crazes-through-the-decades/. Encourage the audience to participate using hand movements or their feet while still sitting. Give a few facts about the dance crazes.
- Focus on one decade at a time, adding other information about trends and events that happened during that decade.

REFERENCES

Gorlinski, Gine, ed. 2010. *The 100 Most Influential Musicians of All Time*. New York: Britannica Educational Publishing.
Leight, Elias. October 27, 2014. "The Top 20 Billboard Hot 100 Hits of the 1960s." http://billboardtop100of.com/1960-2/.
Motown Museum. 2016. "Motown: The Sound That Changed America." https://www.motownmuseum.org/story/motown/.
Rolling Stone. December 3, 2010. "100 Greatest Artists: The Beatles, Eminem and More of the Best of the Best." https://www.rollingstone.com/music/music-lists/100-greatest-artists-147446/the-band-2-88489/.
Top 40 Weekly. 2016a. "Top 100 Artists of the 1950s." https://top40weekly.com/top-100-artists-of-the-50s/.
Top 40 Weekly. 2016b. "Top 100 Artists of the 1960s." https://top40weekly.com/top-100-artists-of-the-60s/.

SUPERHERO STORYTIME

Program by Marie Corbitt, Outreach Program Librarian
Westerville Public Library, Westerville, Ohio

Description

Outreach programs for seniors at the Westerville Public Library focus on Remember When Story Times. They have been very popular and easy to adapt for different group levels. Nine programs are presented a month to older adults in independent and assisted living facilities, nursing homes, and memory care centers. A different topic is chosen each month and follows the same format:

• Picture with story
• Some type of interactive activity
• Picture with a story
• Song
• Picture with story or fun facts
• Some type of interactive activity

This is changeable depending on the subject. The following is an outline of the Superhero program.

Supplies/Materials Needed

• Pictures of famous superheroes.
• Real-life story of a superhero in New Zealand who risked his life to save a man in a truck.
• Real-life story about the woman who created the Tiny Heroes programs. Use pictures with kids in capes.
• Picture of Wonder Woman.
• Book: *Superheroes: Capes, Cowls, and the Creation of Comic Book Culture*, 2013, by Laurence Maslon and Michael Kantor. New York: Crown Archetype.
• Pictures of *Batman* show villains.
• Comic book facts.
• Batman theme song.
• Yellow hoopla hoop.
• Two soft sports balls with Batman symbol on it.

Program Instructions

1. Start off with pictures of famous superheroes, and see if they know who the superheroes are. If not, I tell them and talk about them just a little bit. For example, this is the Flash, and he's called that because he can run really fast, like a flash!
2. Read about a real-life superhero. I found a story online about a teenager in New Zealand who risked his life to save a man whose truck was teetering on the edge of a cliff. I showed a picture of the truck on the cliff.
3. Show a picture of Wonder Woman, and read a brief story about why her character was created (from the book *Superheroes: Capes, Cowls, and the Creation of Comic Book Culture* by Laurence Maslon and Michael Kantor).

4. Ask if anyone ever watched the *Wonder Woman* TV show and, if so, what are some of the things Wonder Woman had? For example, her bullet proof arm guards, her invisible airplane, and her lasso of truth.

5. I brought a yellow hoopla hoop and pretend it's my lasso of truth! I tell them that's what it is and that I will lasso them, if they let me, and they have to answer a question honestly. At first, that makes them nervous, but I tell them they are easy, nonpersonal questions having to do with superheroes. Here are some examples:

    a. Would you rather have superstrength or superintelligence?

    b. Would you rather be able to control fire or water and ice?

    c. Would you rather be able to fly or have superspeed?

    d. Would you rather be born with superpowers or get them later in life?

    e. Would you rather be a well-known superhero or have a secret identity?

    f. Would you rather fight crime on your own or with a team?

    g. Would you rather be able to communicate with animals or read minds?

    h. Would you rather wear a cape or a mask?

6. I have more pictures for random comic book facts. For example, I have a picture of Captain Marvel Junior and ask if his haircut looks familiar. It should! Because Elvis Presley was a big fan of that character, and the creator based his haircut on him—so things like that.

7. I read another short story about a real-life superhero. This one is about a lady named Robyn who started something called Tiny Superheroes. She makes capes for kids fighting illness and disease. I found that story online, and I show a picture of kids in the capes.

8. Play the theme song from Batman, and have participants guess what the song is from. From the same book I used for Wonder Woman, I talk a little bit about this background.

9. I printed and laminated pictures of *Batman* TV show villains ahead of the program and put points on them. I have two soft sports balls and tape the bat symbol on them. Depending on where people are sitting, I put the pictures either on a table or on the floor and have participants throw or roll the balls on the pictures to get points.

10. This particular story time didn't have as much music. There aren't really any sing-along songs for superheroes that I could think of. But I do often have a sing-along song as well, with lyrics in large print.

Suggestions/Tips for Interacting with Residents

• Try to think of a way to involve everyone like using the hoopla hoop.

• Include motor skill activities. Ball throwing works well for groups that have differing abilities. The activity can be made easier or harder depending on the abilities of the participants.

• Remember When Story Times work really well, especially with the cooperation of the activities director. Having them on board to round up people is key.

• A lot of the stories usually come from the *Reminisce* magazine. It's a really great resource for stories from their time. Try to keep stories pretty short.

• Every now and then, use a picture book but only if it's really good.

• This story time formula seems to work really well. I wasn't sure how people would react to the "lasso of truth," but it's actually really great. Sometimes, if I ask a question to the whole room, nobody will answer, but by singling them out with my "lasso" (I always ask first), it really gets people to talk who normally wouldn't. And some of them have talked more than I've ever heard before!

THANKSGIVING MEMORIES

Program by Phyllis Goodman

Description

Thanksgiving is a special time for family and friends to gather together and enjoy traditional foods and activities that have been passed down through the years. This program includes discussion questions, stories, and Thanksgiving trivia. A PowerPoint slide show was used to play the game of Thanksgiving Day Fact or Fiction. Instead of reading a story from book, I showed the Thanksgiving episode from *The Carol Burnett Show*. An episode from the Jack Benny show—*No Place Like Home*—was also played.

Supplies/Materials Needed

- Thanksgiving poem by Edgar A. Guest
- *Carol Burnett Show*: The Lost Episodes DVD, Vol. 2, Episode 7—Thanksgiving
- Thanksgiving Day Fact or Fiction game.
- Jack Benny (book on CD): *No Place Like Home*—How Jack and the Gang spent Thanksgiving, 2013, Classic Radio Comedy.

Program Instructions

1. Arrive early to set up equipment and to organize your material for the program. Greet residents as they enter the room or finish up an activity.

2. Seat the residents in a circle or around a table so they can see the slide show. Prepare the slides so that the photos are large and clear enough to see. Use a large font for text on the slide, and keep the information brief. Speak in a clear voice, and check once in a while that the audience can hear you.

3. Introduce the theme. Start the program with questions about the audience's family Thanksgiving traditions:

   a. How did your family celebrate Thanksgiving?

   b. How many generations gathered to celebrate the holiday?

   c. What traditions did you continue with your own children?

   d. What is your favorite Thanksgiving tradition or food?

   e. Did you go to a special parade or watch one on TV?

   f. Did you watch football games or go shopping the day after?

4. Read the Thanksgiving poem by Edgar A. Guest, written in 1917. It is available at https://www.poetryfoundation.org/poems/44319/thanksgiving-56d2235de3a16 (Guest, 2019).

5. Play a clip from *The Carol Burnett Show: The Lost Episodes*, Vol. 2, Episode 7—Thanksgiving.

6. Thanksgiving Fact or Fiction game:

   a. Before the program create the Thanksgiving Fact or Fiction quiz using a PowerPoint slide show. The word "Fact" or "Fiction" appears on each slide with a Thanksgiving picture and a relevant statement.

   b. Show each slide to the group and read the statement. Ask them whether the statement is a fact or fiction. Share the correct answer and some brief information (information for this game was taken from History Channel, 2016).

   c. Questions and answers for Thanksgiving Fact or Fiction.

Thanksgiving is always celebrated on the last Thursday of November.

Fiction. President Abraham Lincoln, in 1863, designated the last Thursday in November as a national day of Thanksgiving. In 1939, the National Retail Dry Goods Association asked President Franklin Roosevelt to celebrate the holiday only on the fourth Thursday in November to increase the shopping season. It was made official in 1941.

One of America's Founding Fathers suggested that the turkey should be the named the national bird of the United States.

Fact. In 1784, Benjamin Franklin suggested the wild turkey would be a more appropriate national symbol than the bald eagle. He felt that the turkey was a respectable bird, a bird of courage and an original native of America.

Abraham Lincoln became the first American president to issue a national day of Thanksgiving.

Fiction. George Washington, John Adams, and James Madison all encouraged Americans to observe days of thanks, for good fortune and important events.

Macy's was the first American department store to sponsor a Thanksgiving parade.

Fiction. Gimbel's department store in Philadelphia sponsored a parade in 1920. In 1924, the Macy parade soon became a holiday tradition and the official start of the holiday season. The parade became more popular after it was featured in the film *Miracle on 34th Street.* The parade included floats, giant balloons, Broadway cast members, and the famous city hall Rockettes.

Turkeys are slow-moving birds and are not able to fly.

Fiction (kind of). Domesticated turkeys that are eaten on Thanksgiving cannot fly and move slowly. Wild turkeys are smaller and lighter. They can fly for short distances and have better hearing and eyesight than domestic turkeys.

Native Americans used cranberries, often a Thanksgiving tradition, for cooking as well as medicinal reasons.

Fact. According to the Cape Cod Cranberry Growers' Association, cranberries were used in a variety of foods by Native Americans. Cranberries were also used as medicine to treat wounds and as a dye for fabric.

The way that turkeys move inspired a ballroom dance.

Fact. The turkey trot was based on the turkey's short, jerky steps and became popular during the late nineteenth and early twentieth centuries in the United States. It was simple and required little instruction. It was followed by such dances as the fox-trot and the bunny hug.

On Thanksgiving Day in 2007, two turkeys were the grand marshals for the Disney parade.

Fact. President George W. Bush granted a pardon to two turkeys, named May and Flower, in 2007. The two turkeys served as grand marshals for the Disney World Thanksgiving parade. The tradition began informally when Abraham Lincoln gave a pardon to his son Tad's pet turkey. President Harry Truman made it official in 1947.

Eating turkey makes you sleepy.

> **Fact.** Turkey does contain the essential amino acid tryptophan, a natural sedative, but so do a lot of other foods. It is more likely that the combination of fats, carbohydrates, and alcohol makes people sleepy on Thanksgiving Day.

Watching football on Thanksgiving began with the first National Football League game on the holiday in 1934.

> **Fiction.** The American Intercollegiate Football Association held its first championship game on Thanksgiving Day in 1876. By the 1890s many college and high school games were played on Thanksgiving Day. In 1934, the Detroit Lions played the Chicago Bears at the University of Detroit. Since then, the Lions game is always played on Thanksgiving Day.

7. Play the *Jack Benny Thanksgiving Show: How the Gang Spent Thanksgiving*. This show is on the CD (*Jack Benny: No Place Like Home*, 2013).

Suggestions/Tips for Interacting with Residents

- Be aware that the holiday season may be a time of sadness for some participants. Encourage them to sit and listen if they don't want to participate.
- The Thanksgiving Fact or Fiction game can also be written on cardstock and laminated to pass around the room.
- Ask questions during the program to keep discussion going. Don't worry if the conversation gets off track as long as everyone is participating. Sometimes these comments make for a good conversation.

Program Variations

- Prepare a slide show of some of the balloons and floats from Macy's Thanksgiving parade. Share some of the history of the parade.
- Check *Reminisce* magazine for short Thanksgiving stories.

REFERENCES

Carol Burnett Show: The Lost Episodes. DVD. Vol. 2, Episode 7—Thanksgiving, 1970.

Guest, Edgar A. 2019. "Thanksgiving Poem." https://www.poetryfoundation.org/poems/44319/thanksgiving-56d2235de3a16.

History.com Editors. 2016. "Thanksgiving: Fact of Fiction." A&E Television Networks. https://www.history.com/topics/thanksgiving/thanksgiving-quiz.

Jack Benny: No Place like Home (CD), "How the Gang Spent Thanksgiving," 2013.

TV TRIVIA: *THE GOLDEN GIRLS*

Program by Phyllis Goodman

Description

The Golden Girls Trivia game was created as an in-library trivia night program by teen librarian Judith Wright at Homewood Public Library, Homewood, Alabama. After asking for permission to use the program, I modified the program so it was easier to use with residents living in a nursing home. Ms. Wright created the questions for the game by watching the *Golden Girls* episodes and using the *Thank You for Being a Friend* trivia book by Michael Craig. The game was put on a PowerPoint slide show and shown on a large screen. Each slide has a picture or quote from the show and a question. There are five rounds in the game and two bonus rounds. Each round has five questions and a slide with the answers. The main activity of this program is the Jeopardy-style trivia game. However, fun facts about the show are shared and music is included.

Supplies/Materials Needed

- *Golden Girls* TV series
- Pictures of the main characters printed on cardstock or shown on the computer
- "Thank You for Being a friend" theme song printed in large font on poster board or put on a computer monitor
- Quick facts about the *Golden Girls* series, https://goldengirlscentral.com
- PowerPoint slide show with questions and answers
- Score sheet
- Small prizes such as library swag or books

Program Instructions

1. Arrive early to set up the equipment and to organize your materials. Greet participants as they enter the room or finish up a previous activity.
2. Seat participants in a semicircle or around a table so they can see the slide show or other material that is being shown.
3. Introduce the theme, and ask how many ever watched the *Golden Girls* TV show that was televised from 1985 through 1992. Ask participants who their favorite character is and why.
4. Prepare pictures of the main characters before the program and show to the group one at a time. Ask participants who the character is and what they remember about that character. Share some facts about each character. (Information for this activity can be found on Golden Girls Central, which has information about the characters and the show: https://goldengirlscentral.com.)
5. Display the lyrics to the show's opening song in large font on poster board or computer screen. Encourage the group to sing along.
6. Play the Golden Girls Trivia game.

   a. Create the slide show before the program with questions and answers about the show. Each slide has a picture or quote from the show with a question. There are five rounds, and each round has five questions. The answers are shown at the end of each round, with a bonus round at the end. The questions were created by Judith Wright, Homewood Public Library, using the *Golden Girls Trivia Book* by Michael Craig and by watching the show.

b. Divide the group into teams of two or three, and give each group a score sheet. Have each team choose someone to write down the answers on the score sheet.

Golden Girls **TV Show Trivia Questions**

Round One—Each question is worth one point

1. Dorothy brought Sophia to live with her when a fire burned the retirement home she was living in called _____?
2. What fairytale story do the Golden Girls perform in a play?
3. St. Olaf was located in what state?
4. Dr. _____ lived next door to the Golden Girls.
5. "The older you get, the better you get, unless you're a _____."

Answers

1. Shady Pines; 2. Henny Penny; 3. Minnesota; 4. Harry Weston; 5. Banana

Round Two—Each question is worth two points

1. Why didn't Blanche marry Harry in the first show?
2. Rose's kidnapped teddy bear was named?
3. When Stan's Czech cousin, Magda, visited America, what did she say was the best thing about the United States?
4. Blanche's place of employment was where?
5. Who said, "I finally coaxed her out with a pork chop"?

Answers

1. He was already married; 2. Fernando; 3. Slupees; 4. A museum; 5. Sophia

Round Three—Questions are worth three points each

1. One of Rose's favorite words is "videnfrugen." What is a "videnfrugen"?
2. Sophia claimed to have an affair with this world leader?
3. Who did Rose fantasize was her father?
4. What famous 1980s' celebrity do the golden girls want to meet in Miami?
5. Sophia claimed that she was a friend and former business partner with this family Italian chef?

Answers

1. Servant; 2. Winston Churchill; 3. Bob Hope; 4. Burt Reynolds; 5. Mama Celeste

Round Four—Questions are worth four points each

1. What is Rose's birth father's profession?
2. Which actress was a costar on *Mama's Family* with Vicki Lawrence?
3. As part of a *Golden Girls* spinoff, Dr. Harry Weston starred in what TV show?
4. What did Rose's adoptive parents want her to be when she grew up?
5. Which actress was on the sitcom *Maude*?

Answers

1. A monk; 2. Both Betty White and Rue McClanahan; 3. Empty nest; 4. Champion ice skater; 5. Both Rue McClanahan and Bea Arthur

Round Five—Questions are worth five points each

1. What kind of car was Dorothy "knocked" up in?
2. What is the name of the cook who only appeared in the pilot episode?
3. Dorothy's brother was never seen on the show. What was his name?
4. What award was Rose honored with in St. Olaf?
5. This gadget was invented by Stanley. It allowed a person to open up a hot potato without burning their fingers.

Answers

1. Studebaker; 2. Coco; 3. Phil; 4. St. Olaf's Woman of the Year; 5. The Zborni.

   Bonus Question—One question with two answers. Each correct answer is worth five points.

1. What two books does Dorothy want Stan's Czech cousin, Magda, to read?

Answer(s):

Common Sense by Thomas Paine
Vanna White's autobiography, *Vanna Speaks*

Suggestions/Tips for Interacting with Residents

• Face the group when reading the questions and speak clearly.
• Prepare the slides so that the photos are large and clear enough to see. Use a large font for text on the slide, and keep the information brief.
• Speak in a clear voice, and check once in a while that the audience can hear you.

Program Variations

- Create trivia games from other popular TV shows such as the *Andy Griffith Show*, *Magnum PI*, *Friends*, *Gilligan's Island*, *Adam-12*, *Dragnet*, and *Star Trek*.
- Print out a coloring page from the Internet.

REFERENCE

Craig, Michael. July 17, 2013. *Thank You for Being a Friend: A Golden Girls Trivia Book*. Scotts Valley: CA: CreateSpace Independent Publishing Platform.

THE TWELFTH MONTH: THE HOLIDAY MONTH

Program by Phyllis Goodman

Description

December is the twelfth month in the Gregorian and Julian calendars. It is the month with many holiday events and the beginning of winter. Public libraries are sometimes in the position of not being allowed to recognize religious holidays. Also many centers may have their calendars filled with their own holiday programs. This program looks at December and the holidays in a different way. This program celebrates the twelfth month of the year as well as recognizes some holiday traditions with stories and a craft.

Supplies/Materials Needed

- Pictures or slides of things that come in sets of twelve (from ElderSong activity newsletter [ElderSong Publications, Inc., 2012]).
- "The Twelve Days of Christmas." The *Twelve Days of Christmas* by Isadora Rachel
- Holiday stories or books to book talk. At the visit prior to the twelfth month, ask the participants what some of their favorite holiday books are, and bring some of those titles to read. Some favorites mentioned by participants are as follows:
  - *The Night Before Christmas* by Clement Moore
  - *The Christmas Story* by Charles Dickens
  - *The Gift of the Magi* by O. Henry
  - "Stopping by the Woods on a Snowy Evening" by Robert Frost
- **Button tree craft:**
  - Trees made out of craft sticks
  - Precut paper stars
  - Buttons
  - Ornament hook or ribbon
  - Glue

Program Instructions

1. Arrive early to organize materials that will be used in this program. Greet residents as they enter the room or finish up a previous activity.
2. Seat participants in a semicircle or around a table so they can see the slide show or other material that is being shown.
3. Introduce the theme, and begin with some interesting questions about the number twelve (from "December, The Twelfth Month Activity Newsletter," November 1, 2012. Copyright ElderSong Publications, Inc. Used by permission).
   a. Were you born on the twelfth day of the month? Was anyone in your family?
   b. Do you know a family with twelve children?

From On the Go with Senior Services: Library Programs for Any Time and Any Place *by Phyllis Goodman.*
Santa Barbara, CA: Libraries Unlimited. Copyright © 2020.

c. Have you ever cooked for twelve children?

d. Did you ever watch *Adam-12* on TV?

e. Did you watch the movie *Twelve Angry Men*?

f. Have you ever attended a noon wedding?

g. Did you ever stay up until midnight on New Year's Eve?

h. Did you ever work the midnight shift?

4. Talk about things that come in sets of twelve—a dozen eggs, the number twelve on a pool ball, twelve inches in a foot, twelve zodiac signs, and so on. Ask the audience for ideas of things that come in sets of twelve. Write the items on a dry-erase board or paper. Add some other items, and share an interesting fact about it. For example, Joe Namath's number was twelve when he played as a quarterback for the New York Jets. He played with them for twelve years.

5. Talk about the history of the song "Twelve Days of Christmas" and the items mentioned in the song. Read a version of *The Twelve Days of Christmas*. We read *The Twelve Days of Christmas* by Isadora Rachel together.

6. At one of the previous visits I asked residents what their favorite Christmas stories were. I brought some of them with me to read and added on some of my own.

7. Button tree craft—This craft works well because some of it can be put together ahead of time.

   • Before the program have volunteers paint the craft sticks green and glue them together into the shape of a tree. Have volunteers also cut tree trunks out of brown paper and glue them on the trees. Purchase buttons of different colors and sizes.

   • Have the participants glue buttons on the tree. For those who are not able to glue the buttons on themselves, ask volunteers or activity center staff to help with the activity. Give each person a yellow star to put on the top of the tree. Attach an ornament hook to the top of the tree.

   • Red or green ribbon could also be used so that the tree could be hung on a door knob or wall.

Suggestions/Tips for Interacting with Residents

• For those who have arthritis or poor vision, have a volunteer or center staff help them complete the craft.

• Ask participants at the previous visit what their favorite holiday book is and try to bring some of those. Add some extra, especially if a particular book is not working.

• Prepare the slides so that the photos are large and clear enough to see. Use a large font for text on the slide, and keep the information brief.

• Speak in a clear voice, and check once in a while that the audience can hear you.

Program Variations

• The purpose of this program is to recognize the holidays but not offend anyone's religious or personal views. Knowing the library's and community's policy about holidays is a must. If appropriate, add some facts about other holidays during the month of December. Create a trivia game or quiz and see how much the participants know about other traditions.

• Create a holiday mystery box. Gather items related to the holidays, and put them on a tray or in a brightly decorated box or stocking. Pass the tray or box around so participants can look at them. Remove the items and ask the group to tell you what was in the box. Write the items they come up with on a dry-erase board or piece of paper. Show the tray again and see how many they got right.

• Share some facts about other holiday traditions such as Christmas cards and trees, Hanukah, or Kwanzaa.

REFERENCE

ElderSong Publications, Inc. November 1, 2012. "December, The Twelfth Month Activity Newsletter," blog. https://blog.eldersong.com/2012/11/the-number-twelve/.

VALENTINE'S DAY

Program by Phyllis Goodman

Description

Valentine's Day may bring back memories of creating and passing out valentine cards to classmates and friends. As an adult it may bring back memories of a first love. This program explores some of the history about Valentine's Day and includes love stories, poems, and games.

Supplies/Materials Needed

- *Chicken Soup for the Soul: Love Stories* by Jack Canfield
- Book—*Twosomes* by Marilyn Singer
- Valentine's Day trivia
- *Shakespeare's Love Sonnets* by Caitlin Keegan
- PowerPoint slide showing the history of Valentine's Day
- Conversation hearts
- Yes and no questions to use with the conversation hearts game

Program Instructions

1. Arrive early to organize materials that will be used with this program. Greet residents as they enter the room or finish up a previous activity.
2. Seat participants in a semicircle or around a table so they can see the slide show or other material that is being shown.
3. Introduce the theme, and begin with some discussion questions such as follows:

   a. Did you pass out Valentine's Day cards in school as a child?

   b. How did you celebrate as an adult?

   c. Did you go out to a special restaurant?

   d. Did you get/give special candy for Valentine's Day?

4. Read some of *Shakespeare's Love Sonnets*, and share the book *Twosomes* by Marilyn Singer. The book *Twosomes* is a juvenile (not childish) book that is humorous and fun to read. The pictures can be shown on the computer as the story is read.
5. Read a selection from *Chicken Soup for the Soul: Love Stories* by Jack Canfield.
6. Prepare a PowerPoint slide show about the history of Valentine's Day (information for this activity was taken from these resources: Davis, 2018; Levine, 2012).

   a. Begin the slide show with pictures of Valentine's Day cards from over the years. Ask the audience if they or someone in their family received a similar card.

   b. The history of Valentine's Day is not clear, but this version is the most accepted. Juno, the goddess of marriage, was honored by Romans, with a feast on February 14. The legend continues that the next day a festival was held for the god of fertility Lupercus (Lupercalian tradition). This festival matched unmarried men and women in a lottery system, who would remain together for a year. Many ended up marrying at the end of the year. This tradition was banned when Emperor Claudius II found that married men did not want to leave their wives and children to fight in a battle.

c. The ban did not stop people from wanting to be married. A priest named Valentinus (Valentine) secretly performed marriages and was eventually thrown in jail and beheaded on February 14, 270. It is believed that Pope Gelasius two hundred years later made Valentinus a martyred saint and created St. Valentine's Day to replace previous traditions.

d. The English version of the Lupercalian festival was more romantic. An unmarried soldier or knight would draw a name of an unmarried maiden from a basket, draw hearts around it, and pin it to his sleeve.

e. Romance associated with St. Valentine's Day came much later. Geoffrey Chaucer's poem written to commemorate Richard II's engagement linked the day to birds and romance.

f. In 1537, Valentine's Day was made an official holiday by King Henry VIII of England, but it was not celebrated as a day of love until the 1600s. Valentine's Day is celebrated in much the same way in the United States and Britain, while some countries add their own customs to celebrate the day.

g. The Danish exchange poetry and candy snowdrops.

h. In Japan, two kinds of chocolate (giri-choco and honmei-choco) are exchanged. Only women hand out chocolate on February 14. Men give out white chocolate to the women in their lives on March 14 (White Day). More than 50 percent of chocolate sales in Japan are for Valentine's Day.

i. In South America roses, chocolates, and other gifts are exchanged. In addition, men celebrate by serenading their loved one with songs.

j. The rose was the favorite flower of the goddess of love, Venus, and is considered a symbol of romance. However, in Peru and Colombia, orchid bouquets are given instead of roses. Colombia exports the majority of Valentine's Day flowers, with at least thirty flights a day flown from Colombia to the United States during the first two weeks of February.

k. In Wales the tradition of carving a wooden spoon with ornate symbols to express one's feelings and intentions goes back centuries.

l. Over 50 percent of Valentine's Day cards are bought in the six days before the holiday, not including e-cards. More e-cards are sent for Valentine's Day than for any other holiday. In 2010, about fifteen million e-cards were sent. Twenty-five percent of all cards are sold on Valentine's Day, second to Christmas.

m. In the eighteenth and nineteenth centuries, handwritten valentines were exchanged. In the mid-1800s a new style of Valentine's Day card became very popular and was mass produced. Paper lace and intricate designs of cupid, flowers, birds, and hearts were often added to the card. They were often trimmed with ribbons, satin, or dried flowers. As the eighteenth- and nineteenth-century cards became mass produced, they took on more shapes and designs.

n. The tradition of giving chocolates on Valentine's Day is relatively new. The tax on sugar was abolished in 1874, and sugar became more affordable. Sugar consumption increased, and candies and sweets were given as gifts. In the 1890s shopkeepers were selling heart-shaped boxes of candies along with Valentine's Day cards. By the early 1900s heart-shaped boxes of chocolates given on Valentine's Day was a tradition.

o. NECCO produced conversation hearts in 1902. They were larger than a dime and contained longer messages. But in time, the messages became shorter and the hearts smaller.

7. Conversation heart game:

a. For this game I cut hearts out of cardstock paper and wrote a message on them. I used messages that would work as a response to a "yes" or "no" question, such as "Let it be," "Be good," "Yes dear," "Yes," and "You wish."

b. The hearts were placed in a basket. Before the program, I made a list of nonpersonal questions that could be answered as "yes" or "no." Questions such as "Will it rain this week?" or "Will you eat pizza tonight?" work well.

c. I went around the room and asked each person who wanted to participate a question: he or she picked a heart out of the basket to use to answer my question.

Suggestions/Tips for Interacting with Residents

- Prepare the slides so that the photos are large and clear enough to see. Use a large font for text on the slide, and keep the information brief.
- Speak in a clear voice, and check once in a while that the audience can hear you.
- If someone does not want to play the game, that is okay. Encourage them to stay and enjoy the game without playing.
- Explain that the conversation heart game is just for fun and the questions are not meant to be personal.

Program Variations

- An alternative to the conversation heart game would be to cut large hearts out of paper and write a message such as "Yes," "No," and "Let's go" on each one. Tape the hearts to the floor or wall. Tape hearts to soft balls. Read the "yes" or "no" questions, and taking turns, ask each participant to answer the question by throwing the ball at the heart that has their answer.
- Check with the activity center first as to what treats participants may have. Bring some conversation hearts or sweets to share. Or ask the activity center to have something special for Valentine's Day.

REFERENCES

Davis, Kathleen, and Nicol Natale. December 12, 2018. "18 Valentine's Day Facts You Probably Didn't Know." https://www.womansday.com/relationships/a4702/10-fun-valentines-day-facts-103385/.

Levine, Deborah. 2012. *Love Miscellany: Everything You Always Wanted to Know about the Many Ways We Celebrate Romance and Passion.* New York: Skyhorse Publishing.

CHAPTER 4

PLACES AND PUZZLES

INTRODUCTION

The programs in this chapter include programs about traveling and solving puzzles and mysteries. The road trip program includes books, pictures, trivia, activities, nostalgia, and reminiscing activities about family vacations. An imaginary trip to the Caribbean by cruise ship is meant to be a fun trip from the warmth of one's chair. Solving puzzles or mysteries is a favorite activity for many. The mystery and detective program includes a discussion of the popular detective and mystery genre complete with books, games, and puzzles.

Some libraries are experimenting with the use of virtual reality in programming. In Chapter 8, "Technology Connections," Carroll County Public Library staff shares their experience with using this technology with travel and other programs.

CRUISING THE CARIBBEAN

Program by Phyllis Goodman

Description

It is always fun to travel somewhere warm in the winter, and traveling by cruise ship provides many options. Even if someone in the audience has not traveled by cruise ship, encourage them to share their travel adventures to new places. This format could be used with other travel locations around the world and any time of the year.

Supplies/Materials Needed

- *Desperate Voyage* by John Caldwell
- *All at Sea with Truffles* by Sheila Collins
- Travel books and large pictures of the Caribbean
- Bingo game—balls and cage
- Bingo cards and markers
- Caribbean puzzles—supplies needed—jumbo craft sticks, island pictures (five-by-seven or four-by-six-inch pictures), glue, mod podge, and a craft straight knife

Program Instructions

1. Arrive early to set up equipment and to organize your materials. Greet participants as they enter the room or finish up a prior activity.
2. Create a PowerPoint slide show before the program with slides that relate to going on a Caribbean cruise. Seat the residents in a circle or around a table so they can see the slide show.
3. Introduce the theme, and start the discussion with questions about traveling to the Caribbean or other locations by ship. These questions can help get the discussion started:
   a. Have you ever taken a cruise to the Caribbean?
   b. Have you taken a cruise to any other locations?
   c. What was the best part about the cruise?
   d. Have you ever sailed? Where did you go?
4. Show a map and pictures of the Caribbean islands, food, animals, and landmarks that might be found on the journey. Share two to three interesting facts about each picture (information about the Caribbean was taken from travel books—Vorhees and Clammer, 2015).
   a. The first slide showed a picture of a large cruise ship, and we talk about what activities and food might be on the ship.
   b. Show a map of the Caribbean islands from *Lonely Planet, Caribbean Islands*, and share a few facts about some islands.
   c. There are over 7,000 islands, though fewer than 10 percent are inhabited. The most popular islands are St. Martin, Turks and Caicos, the Grenadines, Virgin Islands, St. Lucia and Antigua, Jamaica, Aruba, and St. John.
   d. Turks and Caicos—Cockburn Town is the capital of Turks and Caicos, where you will find a slow pace and brightly painted colonial buildings that have survived over two centuries.

e. The Grenadines consists of several smaller islands that are connected by ferries.

f. Antigua has gorgeous beaches and natural harbors. It still has a working marina and is home to the world's key yachting centers. You will also see cobbled streets and restored buildings from the eighteenth century.

g. Trinidad is home to one of the world's largest carnivals.

h. The Grand Cayman has a large stingray population. Off the coast of Seven Mile Beach the U.S.S. *Kittiwake*'s final resting place can be found. It was sunk on purpose to create an artificial reef and dive site.

i. Aruba has miles and miles of wide, sandy white beaches.

j. The Bahamas are known for their secluded beaches and hidden coves.

5. Read a selection from *All at Sea with Truffles* by Sheila Collins. This book is for pet lovers with a bit of humor. Truffles is a tabby cat that went on a cruise with her owner. The book is narrated by Truffles, who shares her adventures and life aboard a cruise ship.

6. Share the Famous Caribbean-Americans quiz, and see how many the group can get right (information for this activity was taken from these resources: Caribbean Americans in U.S. History, 2004; Ranker, 2016).

---

a. Outspoken Founding Father, a Broadway play made him even more famous.
   Alexander Hamilton

b. Journalist and author, wrote *Blink, Outliers,* and *The Tipping Point.*
   Malcolm Gladwell

c. King of Calypso, best known for singing the "Banana Boat Song."
   Harry Belafonte

d. American actor, film director, and author. In 1963 he became the first black person to win an Academy Award for Best Actor for *Lilies of the Field.*
   Sidney Poitier

e. American track-and-field Olympic champion who competes internationally for the United States.
   Sanya Richards-Ross

f. American statesman and retired four-star general in the U.S. Army during the Persian Gulf War and former secretary of state.
   Colin Powell

g. Singer, songwriter, and one-time girlfriend of Chris Brown.
   Rihanna

h. NBA player, seven-foot tall, who played and coached for the San Antonio Spurs.
   Tim Duncan

i. Attorney general, 2009.
   Eric Holder

j. Actress who appeared in the movies *Sounder* and *The Autobiography of Miss Jane Pittman.*
   Cicely Tyson

7. Briefly share the story of John Caldwell's *Desperate Voyage* from Panama to Sydney in 1946. This story describes John Caldwell's desperate voyage to reach his new wife in Sydney, Australia, in 1946. Unable to find a ship mate, he headed out by himself, landing in the Fiji Islands after experiencing hurricane-force winds. He finally returned to Sydney and eventually goes back to the Caribbean where he makes a life for his family.

8. Bingo game:

   Instead of using "BINGO" at the top of the bingo board, create bingo boards with the word "OCEAN" at the top. Play the Bingo game in the traditional way but instead of calling out "Bingo" when the game is won, the winner calls out "Ocean" (Bingo game templates can be found online).

9. The cruise ship has returned home. Review the places that have been talked about in the program, and ask the participants what souvenirs they might bring back with them.

Suggestions/Tips for Interacting with Residents

- Prepare the slides so that the photos are large and clear enough to see. Use a large font for text on the slide, and keep the information brief. Speak in a clear voice, and check once in a while that the audience can hear you.

- Ask open-ended questions throughout the program to encourage discussion. Even if someone has not been on a cruise ship, talk about what it is like to travel to somewhere new in a different way. Talk about what they might see, where they might explore, and what food they might try.

- Have magnifiers available for participants with vision problems.

- Maintain eye contact with participants.

Program Variations

- Share one of the itineraries from the Lonely Planet tour guide.

- For a different activity, have the group make cruise ship puzzles. For this activity you will need staff or volunteer help for those with arthritis or vison problems. Have two or three pictures (five by seven inches or four by six inches) that the participants can choose from.

  1. Hand out the supplies for the craft stick puzzle. Jumbo craft sticks work well for this craft. The number of craft sticks that will be needed for the puzzle depends on how big the picture is.

  2. Line the craft sticks up evenly, and tape the sticks together on one side. (Tape will keep the sticks in one place while gluing the picture onto the craft sticks.)

  3. Spread glue onto the back of the picture. Place the picture onto the craft sticks and press down. Let sit for a few minutes.

  4. Spread mod podge over the picture and sticks. Once the mod podge has dried, cut the sticks apart with a craft knife. Have the participants try to put the puzzle back together.

  5. An alternative to making the puzzles during the program is to make them ahead of time and have the participants take turns putting the puzzles together.

- Instead of a slide show or laminated pictures, pass around books from the library collection with large pictures of the Caribbean. Share information about the Caribbean islands while the pictures are being passed around.

- Read a story from *South Sea Vagabonds* by J. W. Wray. Wray's book is similar to John Caldwell's book in that J. W. Wary built a boat and sailed to the South Sea Islands and retells his journeys in his book.

- Read a story from *Chicken Soup for the Traveler's Soul* (2002) by Jack Canfield.

REFERENCES

Caldwell, John. 1949. *Desperate Voyage*. New York: Little, Brown.

Canfield, Jack. 2002. *Chicken Soup for the Traveler's Soul: Stories of Adventure, Inspiration and Insight to Celebrate the Spirit of Travel*. Deerfield Beach, Florida: Health Communications.

"Caribbean Americans in U.S. History." June 21, 2004. https://www.sun-sentinel.com/news/trending/sflcaribbe anamericans-story.html.

Ranker. 2016. "51 Famous Celebrities of Caribbean Descent." https://www.ranker.com/list/celebrities-of-caribbean-descent/celebrity-lists.

Vorhees, Mara, and Paul Clammer. 2015. *Caribbean Islands, Lonely Planet*. Oakland, CA: Global Limited.

Wray, J. W. 1941. *South Sea Vagabonds*. New York: D. Appleton-Century.

MYSTERY AND DETECTIVES

Program by Phyllis Goodman

Description

Whether it is solving a crossword puzzle or a murder, mysteries and puzzles are very popular. This program includes sharing some of the popular books in the mystery genre and the detectives who solve those mysteries. There are activities to see how good of a detective the audience really is and a chance to identify famous detectives. Reading or listening to Sherlock Holmes or Agatha Christie stories is also a fun part of this program.

Supplies/Materials Needed

- Famous Detective Quiz
- Pictures with a lot of activity for How Good of a Detective Are You? activity
- Book talks—Choose a variety of mystery books from the collection
- The *Original Illustrated Sherlock Holmes: 37 Short Stories* by Arthur Conan Doyle or *Sherlock Holmes Essentials*, volumes I and II on CD

Program Instructions

1. Arrive early to set up the room and equipment. Organize your materials so you can quickly get to them. Greet the participants as they enter the room or finish a previous activity.

2. Seat the residents in a circle or around a table so they can see and hear you. Speak in a clear voice, and check once in a while that the audience can hear you.

3. Introduce the theme, and begin the discussion by asking the audience about their favorite mystery authors. You can also talk about the mysteries they read as children. Try some of these discussion starters:

   a. Did you read mysteries as a child?

   b. Did you read *Nancy Drew* or the *Hardy Boys* (other authors)?

   c. Do you still read mysteries?

   d. Who is your favorite author? Favorite detective?

4. Play the Famous Detective Quiz. Read the statement, and ask participants if they know who the detective is? (In addition to work experience, information was taken from Carswell, 2015; Famous Fictional Detectives, 2013.)

---

a. Author Elizabeth George created this British detective. He solves crimes with his Scotland Yard coworker Detective Sergeant Barbara Havers. **Inspector Linley**

b. She lives in Santa Teresa, California, and runs for exercise. She appears in her own alphabet series. **Kinsey Millhone (created by Sue Grafton)**

c. This elderly spinster sleuth's talent for solving mysteries is not welcomed by the "real" police investigators. She helped determine whose body was in the library and lives in a village called St. Mary Lead. **Miss Jane Marple**

---

d. This retired detective came to England during World War I. He helps solve mysteries with his best friend Captain Arthur Hastings and helped solve a murder on the Orient Express. **Hercule Poirot**

e. An eccentric character and quite skillful at solving mysteries with the help of his partner Dr. Watson. Professor Moriarty is his archenemy. **Sherlock Holmes**

f. This detective appeared in a series of mystery books in the 1930s and was enjoyed by both boys and girls. She often helped her attorney father with his cases. **Nancy Drew**

g. This hardboiled lawyer/detective appeared in more than eighty books written by Erle Stanley Gardner. His first cases—*The Case of the Velvet Claws* and *The Case of the Sulky Girl*—appeared in 1933. This detective later appeared on a very popular TV show from 1957 through 1966 helping to clear the name of clients found in seemingly helpless situations. **Perry Mason**

h. This detective started out as a comic strip and then made his way into films. Forensic science, technology, and hi-tech gadgets were used to solve crimes. Most of the cases solved by this detective ended with a shootout. One of his popular villains was "Flattop Jones." A live-action movie came out in 1990 starring Warren Beatty. **Dick Tracy**

i. "Just the fact, ma'am" was a popular quote from this TV series starring a detective who worked for the Los Angeles Police Department. The other characters in the show were Officer Bill Gannon, Sgt. Ben Romero, Sgt. Ed Jacobs, and Officer Frank Smith, to name a few. **Joe Friday,** ***Dragnet***

j. This detective appeared in more than one hundred short stories and novels and worked from his New York apartment. Colorful characters often appeared in his novels and shows. He appeared in the movies, TV, radio, and comic books. **Ellery Queen**

5. Test your detective skills:

   a. For this activity use pictures with a lot of items or activities going on.

   b. Pass the pictures around, one at a time. If a participant has vision problems, provide magnifiers, if possible, or pair them up with someone else who can point out what is in the picture.

   c. After everyone has a chance to look at the picture, ask participants questions about items or activities that are going on in the pictures. For example, Where was ____ sitting? Or which wrist was _____ wearing their watch on? What design was on the vase?

6. Prepare a brief summary of the plot and detective from some popular mystery books. Hold the book up so everyone can see the cover, and ask if anyone is familiar with the author/book. If someone is familiar with the book, ask them to share some information about the detective in the book. If they aren't able to or don't remember, be prepared to share two to three facts about the plot and detective in the book. These are some favorites but in no way a complete list:

   • *The Sins of the Fathers* (Matthew Scudder Mysteries) by Lawrence Block
   • *The Black Echo* (Harry Bosch) by Michael Connelly
   • *The Monkey's Raincoat* (Elvis Cole) by Robert Crais
   • *"A" Is for Alibi* (Kinsey Milhone) by Sue Grafton
   • *Devil in a Blue Dress* (Easy Rawlins Mysteries) by Walter Mosley
   • *Postmortem* (Kay Scarpetta Mysteries) by Patricia Cornwell
   • *The Sweetness at the Bottom of the Pie* (Flavia de Luce) by Alan Bradley

- *Aunt Dimity* by Nancy Atherton
- *Jack Reacher* by Lee Child
- *The Gaslight Mysteries* by Victoria Thompson
- Jacqueline Winspear (Maisie Dobbs)

7. Play a story from the *Sherlock Holmes Essentials* audio book.

Suggestions/Tips for Interacting with Residents

- Have magnifiers available for looking at the photos.
- Ask open-ended questions throughout the program to encourage discussion.
- Pause for a few moments after asking a question to allow time for participants to gather their thoughts and respond.

Program Variations

- Create a mystery box with everyday items and pass around the box. Put everything away, and ask the group to tell you what items were in the box.
- Create a murder mystery game.
- Play a selection of the Shadow: Radio's Greatest Man of Mystery, originally broadcast between October 24, 1937, and May 9, 1948.

REFERENCES

Carswell, Beth. 2015. "Great Gumshoes: A Guide to Fictional Detectives." https://www.abebooks.com/books/avid-reader/fictional-detectives.shtml.

"Famous Fictional Detectives." September 9, 2013. https://writerswrite.co.za/famous-fictional-detectives/#.

ROAD TRIPS

Program by Phyllis Goodman

Description

Road trips became popular as more people bought cars and had more leisure time. Accommodations varied greatly from campers, tents, and recreational vehicles to staying in a hotel with a swimming pool. This program provides an opportunity to talk and reminisce about family vacations while growing up and the traditions that were continued with their own family. This program includes stories, games, and music.

Supplies/Materials Needed

- Travel books with large, clear pictures to pass around.
- *America* published by Shadowbox Press has large pictures with two or three sentences in large type on each page.
- Car bingo boards, bingo chips, and road music.
- *Route 66: The Mother Road* by Michael Wallis.
- Interactive activity—vacation destinations (from ElderSong Publications Inc., 2012).

Program Instructions

1. Arrive early to set up the room and to organize your materials. Greet participants as they enter the room or finish up an activity.

2. There are some activities in this program that require a hard surface to complete, so it would be easiest to seat participants around tables, if possible. Speak in a clear voice, and check once in a while that the audience can hear you. Have magnifiers available to look at pictures and the bingo boards.

3. Introduce the theme, and start the conversation with questions about family vacations that participants took growing up. Some discussion starters are as follows:

   a. Did you ever drive along Route 66?

   b. Where did you stay when you were traveling? Did your family have a tent or trailer?

   c. How much of the United States have you seen by car?

   d. What was your favorite trip as a child?

   e. What kind of souvenirs did you collect?

   f. Did you take pictures?

   g. Did you continue to travel as an adult?

4. Play the "See the USA Quiz" from the ElderSong activity newsletter. Name the state in which each of the following vacation destinations are located (from "See the USA Quiz," Road Trip Memories Newsletter, July 1, 2012. Copyright ElderSong Publications Inc. Used by permission).

Ellis Island/State of Liberty (*New York*)	The Alamo (*Texas*)
Hot Springs National Park (*Arkansas*)	The Smoky Mountains (*Tennessee/North Carolina*)
Myrtle Beach (*South Carolina*)	St. Augustine (*Florida*)
Grand Canyon (*Arizona*)	Plymouth Rock (*Massachusetts*)
Las Vegas Strip (*Nevada*)	Grand Old Opry (*Tennessee*)
Space Needle Tower (*Washington*)	Gateway Arch (*Missouri*)
Gettysburg Battlefield (*Pennsylvania*)	Sears Tower (*Illinois*)
Graceland (*Tennessee*)	Mount Rushmore (*South Dakota*)
Yellowstone National Park (*Wyoming*)	Carlsbad Caverns (*New Mexico*)
Walt Disney World Resort (*Florida*)	Golden Gate Bridge (*California*)
Mormon Temple (*Utah*)	Acadia National Park (*Maine*)

5. Talk about the history of Route 66 (information about Route 66 taken from Wallis, 2001).

   Route 66 history

   a. The number of registered automobiles grew from 500,000 in 1910 to about 10 million in 1920. Due to the increase in the number of motorists, federal highway officials began to develop a numbered highway system.

   b. Route 66 runs 2,488 miles beginning in Chicago and ending in Los Angeles. It crossed eight states, with Oklahoma having the longest segment (400 miles) of the road. It was the path to the West for the "Okies" and the fictional Joad family from the *Grapes of Wrath* by John Steinbeck, who were trying to escape the Dust Bowl in the 1930s.

   c. It is the name of the popular song, "Route 66," written by Bobby Troup after World War II and recorded by many artists including Nat King Cole, the Andrews Sisters, and Rolling Stones. It was also a popular television series, from 1960 to 1964, that followed Tod Stiles and Buz Murdock on their cross-country, job-searching travels in a Corvette convertible. (Show a YouTube clip of the show opening.)

   d. Route 66 was primarily a westbound road as Americans headed west in search of warmer temperatures or jobs. The road traveled through small-town America with its businesses and restaurants until it was replaced in most states by the new interstate system started in the 1950s by the Federal Aid Highway Act. Interstate 40 serves most of the Southwest today and replaced most of Route 66 by the mid-1980s.

   e. There are many books about Route 66 that show pictures of the landmarks along Route 66. Check your library collection and interlibrary collection for books that have large, clear pictures. Pass around the books, and allow participants time to look over the pictures and comment. Ask them questions and encourage discussion as they look through the books.

6. Pass around other travel books from the library collection with large clear pictures of places in the United States.

7. Road songs bingo. For this activity, I selected road songs from several CDs in the library's collection and put them onto a single CD. *The Fun on the Run: Travel Games and Songs* CD by Joanna Cole has a variety of road songs.

   a. Create bingo cards, with names of the songs you are using written on each square of the board. Hand out bingo cards and markers.

b. Play part of each road song, and have participants mark the song they think it is. The first one to complete a row wins.

Some popular road songs include the following:

"Take Me Out to the Ball Game"   "Route 66"
"Mustang Sally"   "King of the Road"
"On Top of Old Smoky"   "Home on the Range"
"The More We Get Together"   "Do Your Ears Hand Low?"
"See the USA in Your Chevrolet"   "On the Road Again"
"In the Good Old Summer Time"   "If You're Happy and You Know It"
"Yellow Rose of Texas"   "Down by the Old Mill Stream"
"The Little Old Lady from Pasadena"

8. Read a selection from *When You Look like your Passport Photo, It's Time to Leave* by Erma Bombeck.

Suggestions/Tips for Interacting with Residents

- Encourage everyone to participate but also let participants know that it is okay to sit and listen.
- Allow enough time for looking at pictures and to talk about the locations.
- Provide magnifying glasses, if needed, so participants can get a better look at the pictures, bingo boards, and so on. Or pair participants up with someone whose vision is better.
- Another option is to create a slide show of locations and landmarks along Route 66 or other well-known vacation destinations.

Program Variations

- Alphabet game: name the state that begins with each letter of the alphabet.
- Have a sing along with some of the popular road songs.
- Talk about other highways in the United States that are well traveled.
- Check the Internet for travel podcasts.

REFERENCES

ElderSong Publications Inc. July 1, 2012. "See the USA Quiz," Road Trip Memories Newsletter, blog. https://blog .eldersong.com/2012/07/road-trip-memories-3/.
Wallis, Michael. 2001. *Route 66: The Mother Road*. New York: St. Martin's Griffin.

CHAPTER 5

WORDS AND STORIES

INTRODUCTION

Programs that include words and stories are a natural fit for public libraries, whose main goal is to promote reading and literature. The library collection includes a variety of formats, and information library staff knows well—stories, poetry, trivia, audio books, music, and movies. The formats used in the following programs vary, but they all combine words and stories, including modifying the summer reading program so that older adults who can't visit the library are able to participate. The well-known Bi-Folkal kits, still found in many library collections, have found new life at Peoria Public Library outlined in the Chit Chat program. Storytelling, another library staple, and using volunteers to present story times in the Word on Wheels programs are also outlined in this chapter.

CHIT CHAT: TRAINS

**Program by Barb Brown, Reference Assistant, and Cari Pierce, Library Assistant
Peoria Public Library, North Branch, Peoria, Illinois**

Description

The "Bi-Folkal" kits were originally created to be used in reminiscence programs for older adults. The kits contained VHS/DVDs, cassettes, pictures, and an activity guide on specific events or themes to stimulate memories and discussion. These kits are still part of many library collections.

The staff at Peoria Public Library went through the Bi-Folkal kits that were still in the library's collection and found that the original goal of the kits was still valuable. Using the original concept of the kits, they expanded the program by replacing VHS tapes and cassettes with thumb drives and laminating pictures. Realia, artifacts, extra facts, and trivia about the theme are included when possible. The Chit Chat program discussed here is one of the programs that were created. Other programs have included television, Academy Award movies, roadside attractions along Route 66, trains, and Vaudeville.

Supplies/Materials Needed

- PowerPoint with train car pictures.
- Props—such as the train order stick—This was the paperwork order that was rolled up, usually with a clearance card, and clipped to the train order hoop and later tied with string to the train order stick. The engineer or conductor would stick their arms out and aim for the opening in the stick and catch the orders in the crook of their arms.
- Trivia and pictures about the special trains—Lincoln's death, Robert Kennedy, and the forty thieves' trains.

Program Instructions

1. Research the topic and decide what information you want to include. Use any resources at hand (Internet, books, articles, files, documentaries, etc.), and save interesting information, pictures, and articles for possible use in the program.
2. Make an outline of how the information is to be presented, and create a PowerPoint slide show. After researching trains and discovering how many different cars there are, it made sense to use PowerPoint slides and build the train from the beginning (with the engine) to the last car (historically the caboose).
3. Presentation of the program—A picture of each car was put on a PowerPoint slide, and information about that car was presented. (The following outline explains which train cars were used for the presentation and the type of information that was included in the discussion.)

   a. Engine: double heading, triple heading, push-pull, and a top-and-tail.
   b. Tender car.
   c. Hopper car: open, closed, wagon.
   d. Flatcars.
   e. Freight cars: When discussing freight cars, car hobos, tramps, and vagrants as well as their differences were discussed. We shared why a person hopped on trains or rode the rails. Discussion also included different slang used for meals—lump, knee shaker, and sit down; the meaning of jungle/camps and jungle buzzard; and finally the roles that the bulls or railroad dicks played in riding the rails.

From *On the Go with Senior Services: Library Programs for Any Time and Any Place* by Phyllis Goodman.
Santa Barbara, CA: Libraries Unlimited. Copyright © 2020.

   f. Dining car: The why, when, and glamor in the early years of the dining car (this included a demonstration of walking to the dining car).

   g. Sleeping car: The Pullman car was discussed as well as George Pullman, the Pullman strike, and how his grave is protected by the family.

   h. Cabooses: Discussion included how they were constructed, why they were needed, and why they no longer exist.

4. The program ended with trivia and discussion about three of the most famous trains: Lincoln's death train, Robert Kennedy's death train, and the forty thieves' train.

5. The program is very laid back, and the audience was encouraged to share at any time.

Suggestions/Tips for Interacting with Residents

- Encourage the audience to share at any time, and ask questions pertaining to their comments.
- Provide props and pictures that are large enough for the audience to see.
- Ask for program suggestions from your audience.
- Talk about noises or smells that bring back a memory (the sound of a car or truck going down a brick street, visiting relatives, or going on vacation).
- Use an informal setting, with the audience sitting in a circle when possible. If the presenters are at the front of the room, sit down so that the audience can be seen.

Program Variations

- Props may vary depending on who is presenting the programs and what works with your group. It was easiest to use a PowerPoint slide show to show pictures by hooking up our laptop to the facilities' TV. This made the photos large enough for everyone to see. For the Vaudeville program, a clip from YouTube was used.
- Choose topics that would be interesting and fun—Use documentaries, the Internet, newspaper clippings, and pictures from the local history and genealogy department.
- Peoria Public Library has two staff members who present this outreach. The theme is researched independent of each other, and then the information is brought together to create a program.

STORYTELLERS

Program by Alyson Low, Youth Librarian
Fayetteville Public Library, Fayetteville, Arkansas

Description

The Storytellers program began as a creative writing program for residents of a local assisted living facility. Initially, fiction-based writing prompts were provided, but the residents preferred to write autobiographically. I switched to using prompts that encouraged recollections of different aspects of their lives—schooling, childhood games and toys, homelife, the impact of World War II, courting, and so on. However, the residents became so frustrated with themselves—fretting that their handwriting was messy (it wasn't!) and not believing they were expressing themselves well (they were!)—that I feared they would stop coming. Thus, the format was changed to oral storytelling, which is described here.

Supplies/Materials Needed

- Topics for discussion
- Tape recorder
- Notepad and pen for taking notes

Program Instructions

1. The format of storytellers was changed to oral storytelling to meet the needs and enjoyment of the residents.
2. The group meets in the commons area in the center of the building twice a month, where residents gather to do puzzles, read the paper, listen to music, and visit. Having the group meet here catches the attention of those walking through the area and who often stop to see what's going on. Attendance at Storytellers increased due to the location change.
3. When the program first started, writing prompts were used. When the format changed to oral storytelling, an initial Google search was done for questions to ask senior citizens for the purpose of preserving their personal histories. I also thought about the questions I used to enjoy asking my grandma when I had her all to myself. Holidays, current events, comments made by the residents at previous visits, and so on were used as discussion starters.
4. As the participants talk, notes are taken by hand. The discussion is also recorded.
5. I have begun transcribing the recordings with the goal of compiling them into a print document for the residents and a digital document for library patrons.

Suggestions/Tips for Interacting with Residents

- As much as I enjoyed reading their work on paper, there's no doubt in my mind that switching to an oral format has been so much more beneficial for them as they laugh and remember together.
- Go with the flow of conversation. Have several topics in mind when visiting in case the first ones flop.
- Be open to letting the residents choose the direction of the discussion. The most delightful sessions were the ones where a topic was introduced, but a passing reference to something unrelated sent the discussion down an entirely different and wonderful path.
- The program length varies depending on the dynamics of the group. If that happens, don't worry about stopping early. Often the longest, most animated sessions revolved around the topic of food.

SUMMER READING

Program by Phyllis Goodman

Description

The summer reading program at the library provides an opportunity to include older adults who are unable to visit the library. By extending the library summer reading program to residential facilities and places where older adults gather, the library can expand its services and programs further into the community. Libraries can also plan a visit that encompasses the summer reading theme as was done in the summer of 2017 for the summer reading theme—Build a Better World.

Supplies/Materials Needed

- Game board to keep track of reading
- Prizes to hand out for each milestone
- Quilt squares from Oriental Trading
- Fabric ink

Program Instructions

1. The summer reading theme for the year 2017 was Build a Better World. A new summer reading software program had been installed onto library computers, which made it easier for groups to sign up for the summer reading program. This was perfect for older adults who could not visit the library.

2. The summer reading program consisted of a game board for participants to keep track of their reading and three milestones. Prizes were given at milestone. The library bought special prizes such as magnifiers, paperback books, and pens to hand out to older adults.

3. I talked with the activity coordinator about bringing the program to the center, and she was very interested in having the facility participate. A meeting was set up for residents who were interested in participating to go over the program.

4. The program was explained to the group, and game boards were handed out. A meeting was set up three times over the summer to talk to the participants about what they were reading and to hand out prizes.

5. While the activity director would have been able to record reading statistics, it was easier for library staff to record statistics for the group. This was done at the end of the summer.

6. Build a Better World activity.

   a. Description: Connecting with your community was a subtopic of the Build a Better World program. There are many ways to connect with the community, and after talking with the activity coordinator we decided to make a quilt of what the residents considered important in their community.

   b. Activity:

      i. Blank muslin quilt squares were ordered from the Oriental Trading Company. The squares were precut and could be decorated with fabric ink. Each resident was given a square to decorate. http://www.orientaltrading.com/diy-operation-cooperation-classroom-quilt-a2-57_9111.fltr? Ntt=diy%20operation%20cooperation.

      ii. This is where it gets tricky because some of the residents had vision problems or arthritis in their hands and needed extra help or someone to complete the task for them. Facility staff and I helped residents complete the task. In some cases we drew what they told us to draw. In each case we explained what we had drawn, so they felt like they were part of the activity. They had a lot of fun with this activity, so it was definitely worth the effort. After the squares were decorated they were sewn together with a fabric backing and hung in the center's lobby.

iii. Other senior centers in the community took on the project in a different way. One center had a quilting group, and they created a quilt depicting different organizations in the community. It was hung in the library for a few weeks.

Suggestions/Tips for Interacting with Residents

- When working with seniors who have vision issues, ask them first how you may help them. When helping with the design, ask each step of the way if it is looking the way they want it too. If they are not able to see it, explain what it looks like.
- Ask volunteers or center staff to help with the activity.

Program Variations

- The summer reading program is a great way to connect older adults with reading and library services.
- Look for activities that relate to the summer reading theme. For the summer reading theme 2018—Libraries Rock! Norwalk Easter Public Library showed the movie *Singing in the Rain* at a senior residential facility.

WORDS ON WHEELS

Program by Carlye Dennis, MLIS, CVM
Manager, Volunteer and Outreach Services
Fayetteville Public Library, Fayetteville, Arkansas

Description

The Words on Wheels program provides weekly story times to aging adults in assisted living facilities. Story times are led by library volunteers who read short stories, sing songs, and/or interact with residents in conversation. Story times last between twenty and thirty minutes, but visits can last anywhere between thirty minutes and one hour. The purpose of the program is to provide a library experience through literacy and socialization for the residents.

Supplies/Materials Needed

- Books, magazines, and/or articles appropriate for the audience. Examples include poetry, short stories, current events, state or local history, area landscape, gardening, and/or bird books.
- Materials for the programs may be part of the library collection, the program-specific collection, or part of the volunteer's personal collection. Volunteers are encouraged to ask what types of literature their audience enjoys.

Program Instructions

1. Volunteers check in with facility staff or the program director when they arrive at the center and proceed to the location for the program. Locations for the readings vary from center to center but usually take place where residents are already gathered (after an exercise class) or meet to socialize (a common area/living room).
2. The program is designed around a twenty- to thirty-minute story time, which is outlined ahead of time for the volunteer.
3. The program is flexible and guided by resident interaction and the comfort level of the volunteer. Some volunteers only read stories during their visit, and others read stories and ask questions to inspire conversation and dialogue among the group. Others sing songs, read poetry, or talk about local history. The program is not designed to have a theme, but volunteers may choose a specific theme during the holidays or may cater to a group's interest such as state history or reading poetry. The volunteer has the liberty to make the experience for the residents as fun and as interactive as they feel comfortable.
4. Volunteers
   - All volunteers who apply go through an interview process and are chosen on whether they are a good fit for the program.
   - We have been fortunate enough that interested individuals seek us out to volunteer for the program (through word of mouth or from information on our website about our volunteer-led outreach programs).
   - If the program needs volunteers, coordinating with the marketing department to market that need on the website, other social media outlets, and/or the e-newsletter is helpful.
   - Some volunteers prepare their own materials (i.e., bring items from their personal collection and/or the library's general collection).

5. Offering a shadowing experience for new volunteers is beneficial for both the new volunteer and the existing volunteer. Shadowing can help the new volunteer ease any nerves they may have, while giving the existing volunteer the opportunity to train someone can expand their feelings of ownership and purpose in the program and experience they are providing.

Suggestions/Tips for Interacting with Residents

• Each center served is as diverse as the residents who reside there. Volunteers have the flexibility to choose specific themes.

• Get to know the likes and dislikes of the group you are reading to. Content greatly influences the enjoyment and participation volunteers and residents have with one another.

Program Variations

• Words on Wheels originally began as an outreach program for aging adults with early onset dementia and/or Alzheimer's disease. A satisfaction survey conducted in 2018 showed volunteers felt discouraged by challenges they didn't feel equipped to handle—primarily not knowing how to connect with residents who were not capable of interacting with them. The feedback was presented to the service centers, and the format of the program was changed to serve residents in assisted living centers.

• The collection for Words on Wheels was originally supplied by our reference librarian's curated lists. Volunteers would choose and check out materials from the library's existing collection. The redesign of the program in 2018 brought with it a program brand, and a small grant was used to fund a specific and separate Word on Wheels collection. Branded bags were purchased and are used by volunteers to carry books to the centers, and branded bookmarks are handed out to the residents and for program promotions.

• The redesign also helped volunteers feel more connected to and invested in the program, because they are now able to interact socially with residents in ways that were not possible before.

CHAPTER 6

ART-BASED PROGRAMS

INTRODUCTION

Programs in which participants gain a sense of mastery over a new skill can lead to feelings of being in control and have health benefits. Librarians may differ on how often they want to only take craft programs to a center, but art-based programs do have a place in older adult programming, especially when the focus of the activity is on the process and not the end product. Combining literature with art greatly expands the library's goal of promoting literature and provides health benefits to older adults.

The programs in this chapter provide examples of all of the aforementioned points. Six Mile Regional Library District modified an in-house adult maker's series program to be used at an assisted living facility. Ellsworth Public Library conducts art-based programs that begin with a book that incorporates the theme and ends with an art project.

ADULT MAKER SERIES: BUILDING A TERRARIUM

Program by Jennifer Baugh, MLIS
Six Mile Regional Library District, Granite City, Illinois

Description

The idea for this program started with our summer reading program series called the Adult Maker Series. Our branch manager wanted to do a terrarium program with participants at the library, and I thought it would be a great idea to extend it to one of our local senior facilities. The facility wholeheartedly agreed and allowed us to do the program. The library covered the costs but did ask that the program be capped at a certain amount of attendees. This amount actually turned out to be the same amount as the facility typically saw during craft programs.

Supplies/Materials Needed

- Two-inch succulents
- Medium-large-sized glass containers (jars, bowls, etc.)
- Gardening soil or succulent soil
- Peat moss
- Small gravel or pebbles
- Decorative moss
- Decorations for terrariums such as glass stones, pretty rocks, miniature figurines
- Newspaper
- Table cloths
- Small containers or scoops for scooping dirt out of bags

Program Instructions

1. For setup:

    a. Place tablecloths on tables, and put newspaper down at each place a person will sit. The newspaper will aid greatly in cleanup.

    b. Divide all the materials equally between tables. We try to have no more than five per table.

2. To make the terrariums:

    a. Put about one to two inches of gravel/pebbles at the bottom of the glass container.

    b. Fill the container a little more than half full with dirt. If you want to add peat moss, do so at this point.

    c. Plant your succulent(s) in the dirt and then fill in around them with more dirt. Try to leave one to two inches between each succulent. This allows them room to grow.

    d. You can now add decorations to your terrarium.

    e. Water the succulents a small amount. You do not want the dirt soaked through, as this can lead to rot.

3. Care of the terrariums:

   a. Water only when the soil has completely dried out, and do not overwater. Succulents will be watered less in winter.

   b. If temperatures will drop below freezing, move the succulents indoors and away from cold windows.

Suggestions/Tips for Interacting with Residents

- Make it very clear from the beginning that the residents will keep the terrariums they make.
- Wear clothes you don't mind getting dirty and that you can easily move in. Between carrying bags of dirt and helping residents scoop it out, you will end up with dirt on you. I was also bending down a lot to talk to residents face-to-face.
- If you can, encourage residents to talk about where they are planning to put their plants and how they are going to decorate their terrariums. The residents we worked with absolutely lit up when we talked with them and asked questions one-on-one.

Program Variations

- An example of a terrarium was brought to the program.
- Library staff provided a small handout that explained how to continue to take care of the plant.
- The activities director was in attendance and helped out with residents who had more difficulty in understanding what was going on.

ART AND ARTISTS

Program by Phyllis Goodman

Description

This program combines the art of well-known artists, a famous art heist, and an art craft. This program starts out with a book talk of *The Art Forger* by B. A. Shapiro and continues with a virtual reality tour of the Gardner Museum, its famous unsolved art heist, and an art puzzle craft.

Supplies/Materials Needed

- *The Art Forger* by B. A. Shapiro
- Information about the Isabella Gardner Museum from the website https://www.gardner museum.org/
- Virtual reality tour of the art galleries where the art was stolen
- Art puzzle craft—items needed—jumbo craft sticks, famous art pictures (five-by-seven- or four-by-six-inch pictures), glue, mod podge, and a craft straight knife

Program Instructions

1. Arrive early to organize materials that will be used with this program. Greet residents as they enter the room or finish up a previous activity.
2. Seat participants in a semicircle or around a table so they can see the monitor or other material that is being shown.
3. Begin the program by asking participants if they like to visit art museums, or have a favorite artist. Ask if they ever heard of the Gardner Museum art heist.
4. Discuss the novel *The Art Forger* by B. A. Shapiro. *The Art Forger* is a novel by B. A. Shapiro about a struggling artist who reproduces noted artwork for an online retailer. She becomes involved with a forged painting that was part of the Gardner Museum collection and leads her into the dark side of the art world and hidden secrets.
5. Talk about the Gardner Museum and some of the artwork in the collection. Use pictures from the website of the museum and some of its art (Isabella Stewart Gardner Museum, https://www.gardner museum.org/).
   a. Isabella Gardner and her husband collected artwork from around the world, especially Italian Renaissance and Spanish art. When her father died in 1891, Isabella Gardner inherited $1.6 million, which she spent on art. After accruing paintings by Rembrandt and Titian, the Gardners began construction on a building to house their collection in the Fenway.
   b. Construction on the building started in 1899 and was finished by the end of 1901. When Isabella died in 1924 she left behind an endowment for the museum with the stipulation that the art must be left as she had arranged them.
6. Talk about the Gardner Museum heist that took place in 1990, and go on the virtual tour of the Gardner Museum that shows what artwork was taken and where in the museum it was located. There is information provided on the Gardner Museum website: https://www.gardnermuseum.org/organization/theft. Thirteen Works provides information about the Gardner heist and also has a virtual reality tour about the stolen artwork (https://artsandculture.google.com/exhibit/gAIyZKoNat4oLA). National Public Radio (NRP) created a podcast about the heist and talks about it over eight programs. The podcast is called *Last Seen* (https://www.npr.org/podcasts/648710646/last-seen).

7. Art puzzle craft:

   a. For this activity print pictures of famous artwork. I made the pictures five by seven inches, but they could be any size. Print out one or two pictures so the participants have a choice, or print out enough so each participant has a different artwork. Staff facility was on hand to help those with arthritis or vision problems.

   b. Hand out the supplies for the craft stick puzzle. The number of craft sticks that will be needed for the puzzle depends on how big the picture is. Jumbo craft sticks were used for this craft.

   c. Line the craft sticks up evenly and tape together (the tape will keep the sticks in one place while gluing the picture onto the craft sticks).

   d. Spread glue onto the back of the picture. Place the picture onto the craft sticks and press down. Let sit for a few minutes.

   e. Spread mod podge over the picture and sticks. Once the mod podge has dried, cut the sticks apart with a craft knife. Have the participants try to put the puzzle back together.

Suggestions/Tips for Interacting with Residents

- Use volunteers or activity center staff to help with the craft.
- Be sure everyone can see the information about the Gardner Museum on the monitor.
- Ask questions throughout the program to keep participants engaged.
- Speak in a clear voice, and check once in a while that the audience can hear you.

Program Variations

- An alternative to making the puzzles during the program is to make them ahead of time and have the participants put the puzzles together.
- If each participant was given a different picture, pass the puzzles around and have them put them together.
- Give a few facts about the artist and the artwork.
- Using books with large clear pictures from the collection, pass around the books and talk about the art and artist.
- The podcast *Last Seen* on National Public Radio (NPR) devotes eight episodes about the heist. The episodes are each about thirty to forty minutes in length, though one of the episodes could be played during the program. If anyone is interested in listening to more, show them how to download the podcast onto their device.

ARTS-BASED LITERACY OUTREACH

Program by Tiffany Meyer, Director
Ellsworth Public Library, Ellsworth, Wisconsin

Description

A different theme or project is chosen for each visit. The activities and books usually are tied to a season or special event and include an art project that will take up the majority of the program. Reading and books are pulled into the program in the form of stories, magazine articles, current events, poems, fables, and books with good-quality pictures. The program outlined here used the book *Frederick* by Leo Lionni.

Supplies/Materials Needed

- *Frederick* by Leo Lionni
- Construction paper (or precut picture mats)
- Feathers (or small pieces of tissue paper)
- Contact paper

Program Instructions

1. *Frederick* by Leo Lionni was chosen because the themes in the book related to colors and wintertime. Before reading the book, it was explained that while *Frederick* is a picture book, it contains a message that is suitable for all ages.
2. After reading the book, the participants made colorful collages using construction paper, feathers, and contact paper.
3. Each person selected the color paper they wanted to use and cut a frame shape from the paper. The frame was secured on top of the sticky side of the contact paper. Feathers were placed on the sticky rectangle in the center of the frame.
4. When they were finished with the project, participants held their artwork up to the light to admire.
5. The group then talked about how the project related to Frederick's ideas and shared thoughts on winter and colors and emotions.

Suggestions/Tips for Interacting with Residents

- Work with the medium you are comfortable with. If storytelling, music, or playing games is your strength, then use that in your programs. "If you are having fun, the participants will pick up on that and will have fun too."
- Librarians may not always know who their audience will be when doing an outreach program. When doing outreach Tiffany assumes that the group she is working with will be a mixture of residents with dementia and residents without dementia and have varied levels of skills and abilities. Any given program will appeal to some more than others, based on personalities and personal interests. Arts-based programs are one way to engage every participant because the focus is on the process rather than the end product.
- Be flexible and be aware of the needs of the group. Have each person "work to their happy place." Tiffany gave an example of a resident who refused to do the project. The resident was invited to just sit with

the group and chat, which she did, and eventually ended up participating in her own way by helping her neighbor sort pieces for the project.

- Provide a safe space for residents to express themselves. Share the message that as long as everyone is using the materials safely, there is no wrong way.

- The act of creating is much more important than the end result. Encourage positive discussion, and make sure everyone is having an opportunity to participate.

- Use nontoxic art supplies and containers that do not resemble those used for eating.

- Volunteers are used often for Ellsworth's outreach senior programs. Fortunately, many of the volunteers know the residents and their families, which makes conversation and interaction easier. Volunteers engage the residents by helping them with fine motor skills as needed (e.g., cutting with scissors) and by talking to them throughout the process. If a resident has limited vision, the volunteer will provide greater hands-on assistance, explaining each step as they do it and getting input from the participant so it is still their own project.

- Talk with volunteers beforehand so they understand your goals and expectations.

Program Variations

- Another example of an arts-based program was a follow-up to a special fishing outing. Books with realistic pictures of fish, including local fish, were brought to the center and passed around. The group shared details about their fishing experience and made koi fish kites using liquid watercolors and diffusing paper.

- Other participant favorites have included the following:

  ◦ An exploration of the history of quilting followed by collage using fabric squares on chipboard

  ◦ "Snow globes" in mason jars made with air-dry clay, plastic woodland creatures, bottle brush trees, and glitter while admiring books with photos of winter scenery

  ◦ Watercolor experiments using salt and wax crayon resist while appreciating picture book illustrations by watercolor artists

  ◦ Card making with oil pastels on black cardstock, cut with patterned scissors and glued onto blank cards paired with a conversation about family

Suggested Resource for Programming

Best Friends Book of Alzheimer's Activities, 2 volumes, by Virginia Bell and David Troxel. Baltimore: Health Professions Press, Inc.

The Best Friends books are recommended by Tiffany as a good resource for programming—Tiffany further states that "for many of the projects they list different ways that people can participate, whether they are in early stages of dementia, advanced or not affected by dementia at all."

Suggested Resource for Tips and Philosophy

Memories in the Making by La Doris Heinly, 2010.

BOOKS AND CRAFTS

Program by Mary Kay Johnson, Adult Services Librarian
Norwalk Easter Public Library, Norwalk, Iowa

Description

The staff at Norwalk Easter Public Library visits the assisted care center in the community twice a month. For each visit six to seven books are taken to the center and book talks are given. The residents and librarian talk about what they have been reading, and then they do a craft. For this program they made bookmarks out of discarded books. Another person drops off books, including the ones requested from the book talk, at the facility once a week.

Supplies/Materials Needed

- Six or seven books to book talk
- Damaged or discarded books
- Washable ink pads and stamps
- Pressed flowers
- Lamination machine
- Hole punch
- Ribbon

Program Instructions

1. Prepare book talks on six to seven books.
2. Greet the residents and ask them what they have been reading.
3. Introduce the books brought for the visit, and give a brief book talk on each one.
4. Cut bookmarks out of discarded/damaged books (plain construction paper works well if someone does not like to cut up books).
5. Have the residents chose a bookmark, and add pressed flowers and/or stamp design.
6. When the bookmark is finished, laminate it.
7. Punch a hole in the top of the bookmark, and tie a piece of ribbon through the hole.

Suggestions/Tips for Interacting with Residents

- Mary Kay has a background in education and art and uses this background in creating programs for seniors.
- Programming ideas can be found in books about literacy-related projects.

Program Variations

- Use Pinterest or Google searches for craft ideas.
- Ask family, friends, crafters, and other programming librarians for ideas.

CHAPTER 7

MIND AND MEMORY

INTRODUCTION

"Dementia" is a term that covers many symptoms that are associated with memory loss and thinking skills. According to the Alzheimer's Association, one in ten Americans over age sixty-five currently has some form of dementia. Alzheimer's disease is the most common type of dementia, and as of 2019 there were 5.8 million Americans living with the disease. This number is expected to increase to 13.8 million by 2050. The number of deaths from Alzheimer's disease has surpassed that from heart disease and is the sixth leading cause of death in the United States (Alzheimer's Association, 2019b).

Dementia is a progressive disease that can last for years or even decades. In the beginning persons with dementia may not function much differently than someone without dementia. In the early stages these persons may still live at home or with a caregiver. They may still visit the library or attend off-site library programs. Caregivers may seek out library staff for information about the disease or for activities that they can do with their loved ones. Libraries play an important role in providing services and programs for this population. Library staff is not expected to be health-care professionals, but it is important for libraries to become educated about this population through staff training and working with others agencies in the community that serve this population (Alzheimer's Association, 2019a).

Mary Beth Riedner, retired librarian and creator of the Tales and Travels Memories program, begins this chapter with information about understanding patrons with dementia. She discusses the stages of dementia and how to interact with this population. Though the focus of this chapter is on persons with dementia, many of Ms. Riedner's suggestions are also appropriate for interacting with all older adults. Ms. Riedner concludes her discussion with information about creating and conducting programs.

Some libraries are beginning to create programs to meet the needs of their patrons who are diagnosed with dementia and their families. Some of these programs are outlined in detail in this chapter. In the resource directory at the end of the book, additional resources and information about working with patrons who have dementia are listed.

REFERENCES

Alzheimer's Association. 2019a. "10 Early Signs and Symptoms of Alzheimer's." https://www.alz.org/alzheimers-dementia/10_signs.

Alzheimer's Association. 2019b. "2019 Alzheimer's Disease Facts and Figures." https://alz.org/alzheimers-dementia/facts-figures.

UNDERSTANDING PATRONS WITH DEMENTIA

By Mary Beth Riedner, Retired Librarian and Creator of Tales and Travel Memories

Introduction

The number of people living with dementia is exploding as the baby boomer generation ages. According to the Alzheimer's Association, one in ten Americans over age sixty-five currently has some form of dementia. As of 2019, 5.8 million Americans were living with Alzheimer's. That number is expected to increase to 13.8 million by 2050 (Alzheimer's Association, 2019b). Add those people living with other forms of dementia, and the statistics become even more alarming. In addition, it has been reported that over 50 percent of dementia cases go undiagnosed (Alzheimer's Disease International, n.d.).

Many of these people and their care partners are coming into libraries every day. There are approximately sixteen million unpaid family members and friends providing care to this population in the United States today (Alzheimer's Association, 2019b). It is time for libraries to take proactive steps to effectively serve this large and growing population. This may take librarians outside of their comfort zone. Those living with dementia often feel stigmatized by the larger community. As information professionals, librarians can play a significant role in reducing that stigma by first becoming educated about dementia themselves and then disseminating information about the disease to the general public.

Dementia Basics

While not pretending to be comprehensive, here are a few basic facts about dementia that may help to dispel some misconceptions about the disease.

Types of Dementia

The word "dementia" is actually an umbrella term. There are many types of dementia.

Alzheimer's disease, with typical short-term memory loss, is the most common and accounts for 60 to 80 percent of all cases (Alzheimer's Association, 2019c, 2019d). The Alzheimer's Association lists the following ten early signs and symptoms of Alzheimer's on their website and are listed here (Alzheimer's Association, 2019a):

1. Memory loss that disrupts daily life
2. Challenges in planning or solving problems
3. Difficulty completing familiar tasks at home, at work, or at leisure
4. Confusion with time or place
5. Trouble understanding visual images and spatial relationships
6. New problems with words in speaking or writing
7. Misplacing things and losing the ability to retrace steps
8. Decreased or poor judgment
9. Withdrawal from work or social activities
10. Changes in mood and personality

See the Alzheimer's Association website for more information on the early signs and symptoms—https://www.alz.org/alzheimers-dementia/10_signs.

Other forms of dementia, including vascular dementia, dementia with Lewy bodies, and frontotemporal degeneration, make up the other 20 to 40 percent. For a quick overview of these and other related dementias, see the Alzheimer's Association's "Types of Dementia" web page—https://www.alz.org/alzheimers-dementia/what-is-dementia/types-of-dementia. These non-Alzheimer's dementias affect different parts of the brain than Alzheimer's does and, therefore, memory is often preserved. Common early symptoms of these other dementias include difficulty with language, behavior, and mobility.

There is a great amount of variability among individuals living with dementia. It is important to avoid the tendency to stereotype these people as all the same. It is commonly said that "when you've met one person with dementia, you've met one person with dementia!" However, for simplicity's sake, the term "dementia" in this chapter will refer to all types of dementia.

Stages of Dementia

In addition to the variety of medical diagnoses, there are other factors that make each individual unique. While dementia is a progressive disease, it can be a very long disease that progresses slowly over years, even decades. The progress of the disease is often divided into three stages—early, middle, and late. People can remain highly functional for many years after the initial diagnosis. When meeting a married couple, it is often difficult to tell the care partner from the person with the disease.

Dementia Facts

Dementia is not just a disease of the elderly, although age is one of the risk factors. There are about 200,000 people below age sixty-five with younger-onset dementia. Some of these are working adults with young families who are affected in the prime of their lives. Nearly a million Americans, 16 percent of those living with dementia in 2019, were between the ages of sixty-five and seventy-four. These ages are often associated with the golden years of retirement (Alzheimer's Association, 2019b).

The idea that most people diagnosed with dementia are living in a residential facility is not true. A 2017 report on living arrangements of those living with dementia indicated that 81 percent of those diagnosed live in the community, while only 19 percent live in residential facilities or nursing homes. Twenty-four percent of those living in the community actually live alone (Lepore, Ferrell, and Wiener, 2017). It is highly likely that many of these people living in the community are still library patrons. This large and growing population could benefit from library programs and services designed to meet their needs and abilities.

Types of Facilities for Those Living with Dementia

There are also differences in the types of facilities where those living with dementia may live. Some may be in independent living facilities with other seniors. It is possible that many may be undiagnosed or in the early stage. There are also assisted living facilities for those who may be unable to live alone any longer and need some assistance with everyday tasks.

Some of these assisted living facilities may be dedicated solely to "memory care" or may have a unit designated for those living with dementia. Those living in assisted living facilities are more likely to be in the mid-stages of their disease, but they can still be highly functioning in many ways. Those in the late stage of their disease process are likely to be living in skilled nursing homes where they require extensive medical care. Library outreach programming can still be of great benefit to those living in facilities, as will be examined later in this chapter.

Interacting with Those Living with Dementia

There really is no mystery about how to interact with someone living with dementia. In short, just follow the "golden rule." Remembering that everyone shares a common humanity, treat them the way anyone would want to be treated. People living with dementia generally want to have positive interactions with others. They respond affirmatively when they are treated as the adults they are, with individual experiences, interests, abilities, and so on. While people with this progressive disease will be experiencing continuous losses, it is important to focus on their remaining strengths rather than on what they can no longer do. Preserving their dignity, self-esteem, and independence for as long as possible adds immensely to their quality of life.

Person-Centered Care

An emerging gold standard for working with those living with dementia is known as person-centered care. According to the Alzheimer's Society in the United Kingdom, the chief tenets of person-centered care are as follows:

- Treat the person with dignity and respect.
- Understand their history, lifestyle, culture, and preferences, including their likes, dislikes, hobbies, and interests.
- Look at situations from the point of view of the person with dementia.
- Provide opportunities for the person to have conversations and relationships with other people.
- Ensure that the person has the chance to try new things or take part in activities they enjoy (Alzheimer's Society, n.d.).

Communicating with Persons Living with Dementia

Many people living with dementia are eager to talk. It has been reported that people living in care homes may experience as little as two minutes of social interaction a day (Science Daily, 2018). Here are a few specific tips that will help when communicating with a person living with dementia:

- Body language is important.
- Look each person in the eye.
- Get down to their level if they are seated.
- Smile and be welcoming.
- Speak clearly in a friendly tone that is not too loud (dementia does not cause hearing loss).
- Speak slightly slower than normal as it may take longer for their brains to process what is being said. Give them time to formulate a response.
- Give just one instruction at a time, for the same reason as mentioned earlier.
- Avoid questions that have a "correct" answer.
- If they appear to need assistance, ask for their permission before helping them.
- Accept their reality, and don't correct any mistakes about facts that they may make.
- Be sure to be an active listener, giving them full attention.
- Try to listen to the emotional content of their comments.

Library workers may be concerned about how to deal with what is often called "problem patrons." By learning to recognize someone who may be living with some form of dementia and responding accordingly, some of these difficult encounters can be ameliorated or even avoided altogether.

Reading and Dementia
Research Studies

One commonly held assumption about those living with dementia is that they can no longer read.

This is a misconception. Professor Michelle S. Bourgeois of the University of South Florida says, "All of my research demonstrates that people who were literate maintain their ability to read until the end stages of dementia" (Freudenheim, 2010). This stereotype may actually be self-perpetuating, leading to the withdrawal by caregivers of opportunities for reading and interacting with books.

While people living with dementia may no longer read the way they used to, there are several studies that demonstrate the value of book and reading programs with this population. A study conducted in the United Kingdom into the benefits of the *Get Into Reading* literature intervention designed by The Reader Organization concluded that "engagement in reading-group activity produced significant reduction in dementia symptom severity" and saw "a contribution of reading groups to wellbeing" (University of Liverpool, 2012, p. 29).

The National Network of Libraries of Medicine funded a study of the Tales and Travel Memories program—http://talesandtravelmemories.com/—an innovative book and reading program designed for those living with dementia in residential facilities that was first widely disseminated by the Gail Borden Public Library in Elgin, Illinois. Study results indicated increased cognitive and social interactions, improved relationships between individuals with dementia and their caregivers, and a lessening of stigma about people with dementia among the volunteers (Lytle, 2016).

New Definitions of Reading

New definitions of what constitutes reading may need to be developed for this population. Individual silent reading of full-length books may not be feasible as people move through the various stages of their disease process. However, instead of devouring full-length, best-seller novels, which many people associate with "reading," people living with dementia can still enjoy and benefit from different types of interactions with reading materials, such as oral reading and browsing.

Oral Reading

When books and reading materials are brought into social settings and people are invited to read aloud, "magic" often happens. The Tales and Travel program is one example. One by one, participants take turns reading a paragraph or two of the folktale, legend, or myth associated with the region being visited. They also take turns reading the "Five Facts" about the chosen location, making comments such as "Isn't that interesting!" or "I never knew that!" Observers, such as facility staff or family caregivers, are often astounded. Each person has been given a paper copy of the story and facts that have been typed in large font with double-line spacing. Those who don't choose to read aloud either follow along with the printed text or listen quietly. Participants are allowed to keep the copies at the end of the program and often share them with visiting family members.

Other written materials (again typed in large font with double-line spacing) have also been used successfully in Tales and Travel programs. Participants enjoy choral reading of poems associated with the destination or repeating a line of poetry after it is read by the leader. Written lyrics to familiar songs from the location (e.g., "Danny Boy" for Ireland) aid in group singing.

Short stories, articles from magazines, or excerpts from classic novels are other possible types of literature that can be adapted for oral reading.

Browsing

Browsing of nonfiction books is another reading-related activity that works well with those living with dementia. Books chosen to reflect each individual's interests, hobbies, and life experience are the most effective. This idea conforms to the tenets of the person-centered approach mentioned earlier. Other suggestions would be books about holidays, local history, or past decades. The key to choosing such books is to find those richly illustrated with colorful photographs. Browsers are often motivated to read picture captions or related text, but it is probably best to avoid those books with dense text.

Books for browsing can be chosen from both the adult's and children's book collections. Using Tales and Travel as an example, selected travel and coffee-table-type books on the country or major cities from the adult collection work well. In addition, books on the history, cooking, art and architecture, culture, and music of the destination can be selected from other sections of the adult collection. Children's books work well with those living with dementia, as long as they are chosen to respect this adult audience. Books with childish illustrations should be avoided, but there are many children's books published on countries of the world or U.S. states for junior high/middle school students that are appropriate. These books are designed to engage readers through interesting facts and infographics as well as maps and photographs. As people progress through their illness, books written for elementary school students may be more appropriate. Increased white space and simplified vocabulary make them appealing; they are also not too long and easy to hold. Experience has shown that being seated at a table is the best way to share books during programs; the books can lay flat, and it is easier for the participants to turn the pages and examine the text and pictures.

One often overlooked point is that browsing through books allows these readers a modicum of control. In most of their daily lives, they have little or no control over their activities, especially if they live in a facility where life is rather regimented. With a book in hand, they are in charge of whether they look at it, what they look at or skip, or how fast they turn the pages.

DESIGNING BOOK AND READING PROGRAMS

Purpose/Goals

When designing a book and reading program for those living with dementia, it's important to determine the purpose or goals for the program. One suggestion for a positive goal is to provide this patron group with an opportunity for *active* participation in activities designed to fit their own pace and individual abilities. Activities that stimulate their cognitive and social abilities will increase their feelings of well-being and a sense of being welcomed by a well-loved community institution—the library. These goals will help to provide a positive emotional environment that will help to sustain good feelings among the participants even after the program ends. It is best to avoid simply putting on a "performance" that allows only for passive observation or designing a perfunctory session that gives the library permission to say that service to this group has been "checked off the list." Designing effective programs takes thought, energy, passion, and respect for those intended to benefit.

Program Topics

Program topics can be chosen from a wide variety of subjects. The travel theme of the Tales and Travel program is only one of many. It is best to design programs based on the needs, wants, and demographics of each local community. Local history, sports teams, historical events, and famous people are only a few of the possibilities. Try to limit the number of topics covered to only one, or possibly two, per program. Less is often more with this audience. It might be helpful to refer back to the person-centered care discussion earlier in this chapter when choosing topics. When designing activities for each topic, it is important to be sure they encompass the various levels of ability of the individual participants.

Supplementary Activities

The use of supplementary activities is helpful to keep participants engaged and to make the program multisensory. Inserting music, singing, and even dancing into the program is an obvious addition. Passing around physical items associated with the chosen topic adds another dimension to the programs. For example, when Tales and Travel visited Hawaii, each person was given plastic lei to wear, and a pineapple and a conch shell were passed around. Associated food items, such as fortune cookies for an excursion to China, are also a fun addition, when approved by the facility. Providing colored pencils and sophisticated coloring pages found for free on the Web can be a simple yet engaging art activity.

Tips for Conducting Programs

Here are a few tips for conducting a successful program. These and other tips are available on a Facilitation Checklist available on the Tales and Travel program website under the "For Librarians" tab—http://talesandtravelmemories.com/wp-content/uploads/2019/04/Tales-Travel-Checklist-11-20-18.pdf.

- Employ the communication tips outlined earlier in this chapter to establish trust and rapport with the participants. This can be done by greeting each person individually as they come into the room with a smile and positive body language, introducing yourself with a handshake, and asking for their name.
- Set up the room to enhance participation. Seating everyone at tables set up in a "U" shape makes it easier for the participants to see and interact with each other and allows the leader to approach each person from the front. Tables also make it easier to peruse books and other materials.
- Keep the atmosphere calm and peaceful by conducting only one activity at a time. If there is more than one leader, they should not talk over each other. Give only one instruction at a time and allow time for the participants to process what was said. Background noises such as televisions, telephones, or other distractions should be eliminated if possible.
- The program can consist of more than one activity, but each activity should be completed before the next one is started. For example, in Tales and Travel, the browsing books should be collected before a singing activity begins.

Evaluations

Evaluating the effectiveness of each program is important in order to improve future programs. It may be difficult to use typical evaluation instruments with this group of patrons. Many people living with dementia cannot express their thoughts due to their illness, but the following questions may help in making an assessment:

- Did people participate in the activities?
- Did they engage in conversation with presenters and/or one another?
- Did they smile and make eye contact?
- Did anyone say "thanks" or "come again"?

It may also be helpful to ask facility staff or caregivers for input about the appropriateness of the program, whether they saw increased participation, and if the positive atmosphere of the program followed through into the rest of their day.

Professional Resources

Librarians need not feel alone as they begin to offer programs to this deserving group. For example, there is a nationwide effort called Dementia Friendly America (DFA) whose goal is to bring together all aspects of a community, including government, businesses, financial institutions, health services, and community organizations, to "foster the ability of people living with dementia to remain in the community and engage and thrive in day to day living" (Dementia Friendly America, 2018). Libraries can and should be a part of these grassroots efforts. A "Library Sector Guide" has been posted on the DFA website, which outlines a wide variety of ways that libraries can participate in this effort. Consult the DFA website to locate dementia-friendly efforts across the country.

Other useful resources include the following:

- International Federation of Library Associations. Guidelines for Library Services to Persons with Dementia, 2007—https://archive.ifla.org/VII/s9/nd1/Profrep104.pdf
- American Library Association—Alzheimer's & Related Dementias Interest Group (IGARD)
  ○ General page—https://www.asgcladirect.org/interest-groups/—scroll down
  ○ Resources by subject—https://www.asgcladirect.org/resources/alzheimers-related-dementias-interest-group-igard/

  ○ Accessibility toolkit—https://www.asgcladirect.org/resources/patrons-with-alzheimers-and-related-dementias/

Conclusion

Public libraries are actively seeking ways to demonstrate their relevance to their communities. Providing innovative services to this growing, yet too-often forgotten patron group is an excellent way to show how the library can be used in unique ways to meet the changing needs of their constituents.

Libraries can start small by offering one or two new services to those living with dementia and then grow their programs as they meet with success. Not only can programs be offered as part of outreach efforts to those living in facilities, but also they can be offered as in-house programs for those diagnosed persons still living at home. Memory cafés, informal social gatherings for those living with the disease and their care partners, are springing up across the country. Often in collaboration with other local organizations, libraries have been found to be a perfect partner to host these events that effectively combat the isolation and stigma of dementia that so many people feel.

Those living with dementia want most of the same things as everyone else—acceptance, respect, meaningful activities, social interactions, and a feeling that they are still part of the community. Public libraries have many resources that can be utilized to engage and entertain this population while stimulating memories and providing social contact. Knowledge and information, the stock and trade of libraries, are the keys to bringing about the understanding and compassion that is essential to improving the quality of their lives and helping them to live "well" with dementia.

REFERENCES

Alzheimer's Association. 2019a. "10 Early Signs and Symptoms of Alzheimer's." https://www.alz.org/alzheimers-dementia/10_signs.

Alzheimer's Association. 2019b. "2019 Alzheimer's Disease Facts and Figures." https://www.alz.org/media/Documents/alzheimers-facts-and-figures-2019-r.pdf.

Alzheimer's Association. 2019c. "What Is Alzheimer's?" https://www.alz.org/alzheimers-dementia/what-is-alzheimers.

Alzheimer's Association. 2019d. "What Is Dementia?" https://www.alz.org/alzheimers-dementia/what-is-alzheimers.

Alzheimer's Disease International. n.d. "Dementia Statistics." https://www.alz.co.uk/research/statistics.

Alzheimer's Society. n.d. "Person-Centred Care." https://www.alzheimers.org.uk/about-dementia/treatments/person-centred-care.

Dementia Friendly America. 2018. "What Is DFA?" https://www.dfamerica.org/what-is-dfa.

Freudenheim, M. April 22, 2010. "Many Alzheimer's Patients Find Comfort in Books." http://newoldage.blogs
.nytimes.com/2010/04/22/many-alzheimers-patients-find-comfort-in-books.

Lepore, M., Ferrell, A., and Wiener, J. M. October 11, 2017. "Living Arrangements of People with Alzheimer's
Disease and Related Dementias: Implications for Services and Supports." https://aspe.hhs.gov/system/files/
pdf/257966/LivingArran.pdf.

Lytle, M. 2016. "Tales and Travel: Developing Community Partnerships to Expand Library Services." http://
talesandtravelmemories.com/wp-content/uploads/2019/03/NNLM-Final-Report-and-approval.pdf.

Science Daily. July 26, 2018. "Just 10 Minutes of Social Interaction a Day Improves Wellbeing in Dementia Care."
https://www.sciencedaily.com/releases/2018/07/180726161125.htm.

University of Liverpool Centre for Research into Reading, Information and Linguistic Systems. 2012. "A Literature-
Based Intervention for Older People Living with Dementia." https://pdfs.semanticscholar.org/b145/5feadc57d
4599c6ec615591e82cc26ca88a7.pdf.

PROJECT BRIDGE

Program by Jackson District Library, Jackson, Michigan

Description

Project BRIDGE (Building Relationships in Diverse Generational Experiences) program was developed
after the Jackson District Library (JDL) observed a growing population was not being served by the library.
In 2017, the library received a Library Services Technology Act grant through the Library of Michigan,
which was to be used to expand programs for older adults and their caretakers in the community, including
those with memory issues such as dementia and Alzheimer's disease. The library connected with those who
worked with this population and who could help identify who in the community would benefit from these
programs and what resources would be most helpful. The programs were promoted through connections
with local providers, caregivers, library patrons, grant partners, and social media.

MUSIC AND MEMORY

Description

This program was inspired by the documentary "Alive Inside" that describes the Music & Memory program created by Dan Cohen. The program provides portable music players, with music playlists to people
with Alzheimer's disease. Jackson District Library partners with the local Jackson Symphony Orchestra
Guild that provided funding for the music players. The devices are checked out indefinitely to persons with
dementia living at home or in a care facility.

Supplies/Materials Needed

- Portable music player storage bag
- Downloadable music account to create playlists
- Headphones
- MP3 players

Program Instructions

1. Referrals are made to the library through care community staff as well as community members.

2. Staff visits with the individual and caregiver to create a playlist based on the individual's interests. The music is then downloaded onto the music player for the person to whom the device is checked out to.

3. A soft padded bag is used for storage, as it is insulated, and should have a strap/handle that can easily be hooked onto a wheelchair. In addition to the music player, there is a charging cord, headphones, directions both in pictures and the written word, and the playlist. Soft-cloth headphones were chosen to include in the kit because they fit comfortably over hearing aids. Ear buds are available if a user wishes to have them. Another option could be a small speaker—speakers are available although not preferred as they do not have the same engaging effect provided by headphones.

4. The device used by the JDL, was chosen because it does not have a screen, holds fifteen to twenty hours of music, and has one port to plug into. The iPod Shuffles have been discontinued, so a different device and system for downloading music will have to be used.

Suggestions/Tips for Interacting with Residents

• The Music & Memory program has been positively received. While not scientific, there have been noticeable changes in those who use it. "Jane," who resides in an assisted living facility, had lost all verbal ability and was rather combative with daily care and at mealtime. With the playlist provided by her daughter, Jane was much more relaxed and tolerant of her daily care. In addition, she actually regained limited verbal ability, such as saying "hi" and "yes"/"no."

• "Joe," who has vascular dementia due to a stroke, immediately smiled and began singing along when presented with his Music & Memory kit. His wife had tears of joy and stated she couldn't remember the last time he smiled like that. He is frequently in the hospital and uses the Music & Memory kit to reduce anxiety and agitation.

JDL ON THE ROAD

Description

This program involves taking the programs that are offered at the JDL library branches to care communities and senior living centers. This provides an opportunity for those who are not able to visit the library to enjoy the programs others in the community enjoy.

Supplies/Materials Needed

• Library programs that have been presented at a branch.
• These programs have included musical programs, history of the community and local prison, professional puppeteers, storytellers, beekeepers, animal handlers, and local science centers.

Program Instructions

1. Library staff coordinates with the activity coordinator and the presenter of the programs to set the best time and date to present the program at a center.

2. Most programs can be taken off-site, and some may need modifications to accommodate the audience.

3. Residents at care communities really enjoy the availability of diverse programming. In the animal program, the animal handler provides a very hands-on experience where the audience can see, touch, or hold the animals based on the individuals' comfort level. For JDL, this has been one of the most popular programs with seniors.

4. The beekeeper program includes a fully enclosed live beehive to observe, and every member of the audience is able to sample fresh honey and make a beeswax candle. The science program includes audience members being able to test various objects with a Geiger counter and the opportunity to play a theremin. Bringing these interactive, informative, and entertaining programs to the senior population is very well received in the community.

TIMESLIPS

Description

TimeSlips is a creative storytelling program that was developed by Ann Basting from the University of Wisconsin, Milwaukee. The program involves the creating of stories by asking open-ended questions and uses pictures that are not familiar to the individual. This method allows the individual to create a story without feeling like they should be finding a memory. This program is used at centers with dementia patients and also with diverse groups, which may include older adults with other needs. This program requires online training through TimeSlips as well as training with the Project BRIDGE coordinator.

Another option is Beautiful Questions, a program taken to independent living centers once a month. The purpose of this program is to allow older adults to reminisce and share memories by asking an inspiring question that allows them to tell their story, their way.

Supplies/Materials Needed

- Laminated pictures 8.5 × 11 inches. The pictures are available from the TimeSlips webpage.
- A facilitator and recorder to lead the conversations.

Program Instructions

1. The general time frame for this program is forty to sixty minutes, once a week. Up to three images of 8.5 × 11 inch pictures can be used during a program. The images need to be images that do not spark a memory of a famous person or event. Using one's own photos is also an option.
2. Show the picture to the group, and ask them to create a story by asking open-ended questions. Take notes during the program.
3. Once the story is completed, it is read back to the group.
4. Every three to four months a book is created with the stories. The book includes the pictures used when creating the group stories. A copy is given to the storyteller, and one remains at the library.
5. Staff or volunteers help with this program by putting together the stories and conducting the program at some centers.
6. The Beautiful Questions program is also part of the TimeSlips program. Held at independent living centers once a month, residents share memories and reminisce, which is an important part of this program. Topics and pictures are shared, and questions are asked that illicit sharing memories.

CONNECTIONS

Description

This program has been created for persons with moderate to more severe dementia who are losing communication skills. The program includes a kit that contains books and conversation suggestions and can be checked out by caregivers.

Supplies/Materials Needed

- Three to five books.
- These kits have included specially selected children's picture books and Shadowbox Press books, which include large photos and minimal text.
- Conversation cards are also included in these kits, with information about how to share these books.

Program Instructions

1. The kits have been created with the help of librarians and social workers to be used with persons with moderate to more severe dementia who are losing communication skills.
2. They can be checked out like other items in the library by individuals or placed on long-term checkout in older adult care facilities in the community.

JOURNEYS

Description

The very popular Journeys program includes multisensory kits that combine sight, sound, touch, taste, and smell to explore other countries and a variety of nostalgic topics. The kits are an expansion of the Tales and Travel program (discussed in this chapter) and the Bi-Folkal kits. Jackson District Library contacted the Bi-Folkal Productions for permission before repurposing the kits into the Journeys kits.

Supplies/Materials Needed

- Books, music, folktales, tangibles, and snack suggestions for each topic.
- The kits are multisensory, so the items touch on all of the five senses.
- Binder with Tales and Travel guide for the Journey topic subject, interesting information about the area (such as the Wieliczka Salt Mine of Poland and Japan's Maneki Neko), and area-inspired recipes or snack suggestion.
- All the materials are placed into a tote bag.

Program Instructions

1. Kits include books, music, folktales, tangibles, snack suggestions, and programming ideas. For example, the program Journey to Spring has a corsage in the kit, and the Journeys to Home has an old-style egg beater as part of the kit.
2. There are currently twenty kits available. These kits are used by activity coordinators at senior care facilities. The kits can also be checked out to any patron, including teachers and homeschoolers.

Suggestions/Tips for Interacting with Residents

- Have a sense of humor when working with residents who have dementia. Don't be offended when someone makes inappropriate comments, criticizes the story, or your hair style.
- Be genuine and the rest will be easy.
- Encourage people to participate, but let them know that it is also okay to listen.

LIBRARY MEMORY PROJECT AND MEMORY CAFÉS

Angela Meyers, Coordinator of Youth and Inclusive Services
Bridges Library System, Waukesha, Wisconsin

Introduction

Memory cafés are social engagement opportunities for individuals living with memory loss, along with their care partner, family, or friends. They are designed to provide a fun, social engagement opportunity for individuals with mild memory loss, mild cognitive impairment, and other forms of dementia. Dementia is defined as "a decline in mental ability severe enough to interfere with daily life" (Alzheimer's Association, 2019). There are many forms of dementia, of which Alzheimer's disease is the most common.

Social isolation is a real concern with older adults and especially for those living with memory loss. Those living with dementia may find that family and friends come by less frequently because they aren't sure how to interact with their loved one, who is presenting differently than their previous self. Social isolation and loneliness pose health risks such as high blood pressure, heart disease, obesity, depression, and even death (National Institute on Aging, 2019). Memory cafés are one way to combat social isolation by providing an avenue for individuals with memory loss to interact with others on a similar journey. While memory cafés have roots in the Netherlands, they can be found across the United States. Memory cafés are held in coffee shops, nature centers, and even public libraries.

According to memorycafedirectory.com, there are over 600 memory cafés in the United States, with nearly 100 held in public libraries. The memory cafés are planned and facilitated by library staff or other trained facilitators. The cafés typically last 1.5 hours and include a variety of sensory-based activities, which lend themselves well to engaging the targeted audience. Libraries often partner with local organizations like the Alzheimer's Association and their local aging and disability resource centers to provide staff training and ongoing resource support for the participants and library staff.

Bridges Library System Memory Cafés

The Bridges Library System became involved in coordinating memory cafés after attending a conference session at the Wisconsin Library Association in 2013 on this very topic. The librarian from Neenah Public Library who presented the program was passionate about offering memory cafés and provided many examples of what they look like and how they benefit individuals living with memory loss. A few months later, several staff members from our member libraries and I visited a memory café held in a public library to gain a better understanding of this program offering.

Following the field trip to participate in a memory café, the group of library staff met to discuss how and whether we could make this work. The four interested libraries were small to midsize and had limited staff and money to take on new programming but decided not to let those obstacles get in the way. Since the interested libraries were located within fifteen minutes of each other, the libraries decided to host the cafés on a rotating basis, making it feasible for each library to participate.

REFERENCES

Alzheimer's Association. 2019. "What Is Dementia?" https://www.alz.org/alzheimers-dementia/what-is-dementia.
National Institute on Aging. April 23, 2019. "Social Isolation, Loneliness in Older People Pose Health Risks." U.S. Department of Health and Human Services. https://www.nia.nih.gov/news/social-isolation-loneliness-older-people-pose-health-risks.

MEMORY CAFÉS: ALL THINGS ICE CREAM

**Program by Angela Meyers, Coordinator of Youth and Inclusive Services
Bridges Library System, Waukesha, Wisconsin**

Description

Memory cafés are programs specifically designed for individuals living with memory loss, along with their care partners, friends, and family. Memory cafés can be held in many different venues, including public libraries. Libraries are a good fit because they are familiar places, so participants tend to be comfortable returning to the library for an activity-based program, like a memory café.

Supplies/Materials Needed

Materials vary depending on the program being offered. For instance, the memory café themed "All Things Ice Cream" included the following:

- Short presentation on the history of ice cream
- Fun ice-cream facts
- Build your own sundae station (dairy and nondairy ice-cream supplies and toppings)
- Spoon decorating craft

Other basic supplies that stay constant for each memory café include the following:

- Write-on name tags
- Permanent markers
- Registration sheet to record new attendees and check off returnees
- Various fidgets, including soft stress ball, tangle toys, wooden puzzle fidget
- Activity sheets: word search, adult coloring pages
- Coffee: regular and decaf
- Water
- A light snack like cookies or dessert bars
- Copies of the closing (song, poem, saying)

Program Instructions

1. Memory cafés typically last for 1.5 hours, but staff will need additional time (3 hours total) to set up, clean up, and complete an evaluation form. For example, if a memory café is set to begin at 10:30 A.M., staff should start setting up the room at 9:45 A.M.–10:00 A.M.
2. Room setup includes arranging tables and chairs, brewing coffee, and setting out light refreshments with plates and napkins. The registration table can be set with name tags, a registration sheet or sign-in sheet, and permanent markers and pens.
3. If using rectangular or square tables for participants, it is suggested to push two tables together and set chairs around the perimeter. This table arrangement allows several groups of participants and care partners to sit together and have conversations, which is one of the main objectives of a memory café.
4. The following is a sample schedule for a memory café themed "All Things Ice Cream" to be held at the public library from 10:30 A.M. to noon.

5. 10:15 A.M.: Ideally, the room, registration table, and refreshments will be set up by this time. The majority of the attendees are older adults and tend to arrive early. Continue to staff the registration table fifteen to twenty minutes into the start of the program for late arrivals.

6. 10:30 A.M.–10:40 A.M.: Allow guests to settle in, get their name tags, hang up their jackets, and retrieve refreshments.

7. 10:40 A.M.–10:45 A.M.: Welcome attendees to the library and memory café. Provide information on where your restrooms are, especially the location of a family restroom, if applicable. This information is especially reassuring for care partners who are there with a person of another gender.

8. 10:45 A.M.–11:00 A.M.: Use an icebreaker to initiate introductions. The icebreaker can be centered around the theme of the café, about the season, or anything that connects people. For instance, "What is your favorite season and why?" Go around the room so each person can introduce themselves, and answer the icebreaker question. For instance, "I'm Angela and my favorite season is fall. Fall is my favorite because I love watching the leaves change colors." Sometimes we find that individuals with memory loss may not be able to answer the icebreaker question, which is fine. Flexibility is key to a successful memory café. Usually, the care partner, family, or friend will answer on their behalf or provide an answer they both can agree to. You may hear a care couple answer, "I'm Bob and this is my wife, Mary. We love the fall because we always go apple picking with the grandkids." We find that the icebreaker questions help people connect with each other, so let the conversation drift where it may. Another attendee may say to Bob and Mary, "How many grandchildren do you have?" or "Where do you go apple picking?" and so on.

9. 11:00 A.M.–11:20 A.M.: Following the icebreaker and introductions, start with an opening from staff or presenter that introduces the theme. In this example of a memory café, the activity and theme for the memory cafés is "All Things Ice Cream." Staff or facilitators may provide a simple history of ice cream and tie it back to the local community or state, such as a local ice-cream shop. Make activities as interactive as possible, even with something like the history of ice cream. For example, you may work in some ice-cream trivia like, "It takes (*fill in the blank*) gallons of whole milk to make one gallon of ice cream." Let the attendees take a few guesses. Consider showing a few short video clips or photos that are in line with the theme.

   The more the audience can contribute and feel engaged, the more they will get out of it. The goal should be at least 70 percent participant contribution and 30 percent facilitation.

10. 11:20 A.M.–11:40 A.M.: Provide a description of your next activity. The second activity tends to be a craft or involved project. It is best to select a simple craft or activity that involves a limited number of steps. In this example, the participants will make their own decorative spoon with jewelry wire, a spoon (used, purchased at Goodwill or other thrift store), and jewels. Provide an example of a finished product, explain which materials are available, and provide a brief demonstration. Provide step-by-step instructions, repeating them if needed. Move around the room to ask if anyone has any questions or could use assistance. Small motor skills may be compromised with the disease progression, so offer to assist where needed. Simple crafts work best.

11. While the participants are decorating their spoons, ask a volunteer to scoop ice cream into bowls. Have dairy-free ice cream available for those who request it. Once folks are finished with their spoons, invite them to come up to the sundae station. Depending on the mobility of your group and number of volunteers available, staff can deliver the sundae to them with the toppings of their choice or provide topping selections at the tables.

12. 11:40 A.M.–11:55 A.M.: Eat sundaes. Sit down with the attendees and enjoy some ice cream and conversation. You can play soft music in the background for ambience.

13. 11:55 A.M.–12:00 P.M.: Make announcements of the next café or other activities that may be of interest. Sing the closing song, poem, or saying to close the café and signal the end of the program. The public

libraries involved in the Library Memory Project always close the memory café with a song or a saying to ensure consistency among the cafés within the project.

14. 12:00 P.M.–12:15 P.M.: Slowly pick up the room's supplies, but try not to make people feel like they have to leave right away. Converse with individual care couples, and allow for socializing among participants.

15. 12:30 P.M.: Room cleanup concludes.

16. 12:30 P.M.–12:45 P.M.: Fill out a program evaluation, submit it electronically to the Library Memory Project coordinator, and file a copy for your records. The evaluation includes quantitative and qualitative data that is compiled by memory project and year.

Suggestions/Tips for Interacting with Residents

Suggestions for another library to set up a memory café:

- Participate in dementia-friendly training in order to learn how to best interact and serve this population.
- Reach out to your local Alzheimer's Association or aging and disability resource center to ask about dementia-friendly business training for your library or community as a whole.
- Partner with the local Alzheimer's Association or aging and disability resource center. Partnership can vary, from distributing your memory café flyers to taking RSVPs for the memory café to attending and connecting attendees with resources at the memory cafés.
- Libraries find that planning a café with a theme in mind is helpful, such as "Herbs for the Senses" or "Around the Kitchen Table."
- The Library Memory Project partners with the local chapter of the Alzheimer's Association, which assists with promotion of the memory cafés and the RSVP/screening for the memory cafés. A staff member attends each memory café to connect attendees to much-needed dementia care resources in the community.

Tips for setting up a memory café:

- Research. Read about memory cafés on Programming Librarian or Public Libraries Online. Download best practices guides on Dementia Friendly Libraries in Wisconsin or Wisconsin Memory Café Programs at www.wai.wisc.edu/publichealth/guides.html. Watch this archived webinar on Memory Cafés and Libraries: The Perfect Fit.
- Follow the Library Memory Project at www.facebook.com/LibraryMemoryProject or www.librarymemoryproject.org.
- Visit and participate in a memory café.
- Reach out to someone who has offered a memory café, and ask about lessons learned.
- Collaborate with a local agency, preferably a not-for-profit, to provide resources and support during the memory cafés.
- Determine your target audience. The Library Memory Project focuses on serving those who are experiencing early-stage dementia, mild memory loss, or mild cognitive impairment and their family, friends, and care partners. The vast majority of the individuals who attend the Library Memory Project cafés are still living in the community, often with a spouse or care partner. On occasion, a person living in an assisted living facility may attend with a care person, but this is rare. Since memory cafés are intended for one-to-one interaction, they are not suitable for large groups with only one care person.
- Try different themes. It is amazing how responsive attendees will be to various programs, whether it is a taste testing, reminiscing, or learning about the benefits of adopting a rescue animal.

- Be flexible. Have an outline for your memory café, but be willing to go with the flow.
- Understand that you are offering something very special and meaningful for those living with dementia and their care partners.

Materials/Techniques for Doing the Program

- The Library Memory Project developed a traveling tote of materials to circulate among the memory cafés, which includes name tags, pens, sharpies, registration sheets, fidgets, a "permission to photograph" sign, and memory café schedules.

Program Variations

- Take this program out into the community to a group of seniors, such as residents at assisted living facilities. Many seniors diagnosed with memory loss or not may have concerns about their memory.
- Memory cafés are essentially adult programs but planned and implemented with sensitivity, so they can be fun for everyone, even those who do not have memory loss. Think of the programs like elevators. While elevators are designed for those who are unable to use the steps, many people who are able to use the steps utilize the elevator.

MEMORY CAFÉS

Description

The goal of the Missoula Public Library Memory Café is to create a safe, welcoming, and supportive space for individuals experiencing memory loss and their caregivers and family members. The Memory Café program is held at the library but could easily be held at a senior facility or on a mobile bus. It is modeled after an international concept created by the National Alzheimer's Café Alliance. Topics for the Memory Café vary and typically allow participants to reminisce about past times or enjoy new experiences. Activities-based experiences provide participants mutual support, information exchange, and the company of those with similar experiences, in a relaxing café-style atmosphere. The following outlines how Missoula Public Library sets up Memory Cafés at the library and some of the activities and topics they have used.

Supplies/Materials Needed

- The supplies used for each program reflect the theme being discussed at the café meeting.
- A guest speaker and/or staff from a health-care organization provides information about brain health and memory loss.

Program Instructions

1. The Memory Café model adopted by Missoula Public Library is currently being used internationally. Information about the Memory Café model can be found on the Alzheimer's Cafe website (www .alzheimerscafe.com). The café provides support to people with dementia and their caregivers. It provides an opportunity to share resources and ideas and to get away from routines.
2. Each month the café has a new theme and activity. A guest speaker as well as a health-care or social services representative able to share information about brain health, memory loss, Alzheimer's disease, and dementia is also present.
3. Topics for the Memory Café vary and allow participants to reminisce about past times or enjoy new experiences.
4. Some examples of cafés that have been done at Missoula Public Library are as follows:

   a. Inviting a local ice-cream store to talk about the process of making ice cream and have an ice-cream tasting.

   b. The historical museum presented a program about one-room school houses.

   c. For the Fourth of July we had a live piano and patriotic sing-along, along with the constitution and Fourth of July trivia.

   d. A local science museum presented a butterfly-observing activity.

   e. Program about healthy aging.

Suggestions/Tips for Interacting with Residents

- By creating an activities-based experience, we provide participants mutual support, information exchange, and the company of those with similar experiences, in a relaxing café-style atmosphere.

MUSIC & MEMORY

Introduction

The Music & Memory program was founded by Dan Cohen who studied the effect of familiar music on the quality of life of nursing home residents with dementia and Alzheimer's disease. Mr. Cohen's program was highlighted in a 2014 documentary called "Alive Inside: A Story of Music and Memory," produced by Michael Rossato-Bennett. Mr. Cohen created individualized music playlists that were then downloaded onto iPods and given to residents living in nursing homes with dementia and Alzheimer's disease. The idea of the program was to use music to help these patients reconnect with the world and help to unlock memories. In many cases, playing music brought back memories for the patient and increased the quality of their ability to interact. Staff could then use this time to interact with the patient whether it was talking with them or giving them their medications. In some cases, using the music reduced the amount of medication needed. The outcome was a success, and the Music & Memory program has been implemented in many nursing homes.

While the original program was designed for use only with residents living in nursing homes, a version of it has been used in hospitals, hospices, home care, and libraries. The Jackson District Library, Madison Public Library, and the Suffolk Cooperative Library System represent three libraries that have embraced the Music & Memory program and have the same outcome for their libraries. However, each library system has approached implementation of the program in a different way.

REFERENCES

"Alive Inside: A Story of Music and Memory." 2019. http://www.aliveinside.us/#land.
Music & Memory Program. 2019. https://musicandmemory.org/.

THE MUSIC & MEMORY PROGRAM

Program by Mary Fahndrich, Community Engagement Librarian, Madison Public Library, Wisconsin, and Julie Hyland, Director, Music & Memory Program, Wisconsin

Description

The Music & Memory program began with a grant received by the Wisconsin Department of Health Services. The grant was provided by the Federal Administration for Community Living to provide startup funding to support the program at public libraries. There are four counties in Wisconsin, including Dane County where Madison is located, that provide this library-based program.

The program funding is intended for individuals who are still living at home in the community; therefore, individuals, family members, or other caregivers do need to visit the library to create their personalized playlist. Libraries do reach out to local senior centers, dementia and Alzheimer's associations/groups, senior apartment buildings, and so on to spread the word.

Supplies/Materials Needed

- Staff training conducted by Music & Memory staff
- Computer
- Startup kits (funded with grant money) included iPods and headphones
- iTunes gift cards
- A place to burn CDs, download songs, and maintain the iTunes library

Program Instructions

1. Staff receives Music & Memory certification, which consists of three 90-minute interactive webinars with Music & Memory staff. At least two staff members from eight of the nine Madison Public Library locations currently offer the Music & Memory program.
2. The grant funds covered the cost of both certification training and "startup kits" for all locations.
3. Once staff training was completed, a kick-off event was held to announce the availability of the program to Madison community members.
4. The documentary "Alive Inside" was screened during the event, and staff from the Wisconsin Department of Health Services and Wisconsin Music & Memory program spoke about the program and dementia-friendly efforts in the state. In addition, the dementia care specialists from the Dane County Aging and Disability Resource Center, the Alzheimer's Association, and the Alzheimer's and Dementia Alliance were present.
5. This is an in-house program; therefore, interested persons need to contact their local library to start the process.
6. The individual and/or family member fills out a form with basic contact information as well as a survey about musical interests. This information helps determine what music is most meaningful to the person with dementia and helps to create playlists of music that reflect their tastes, interests, and background.
7. In some cases the initial form is filled out in advance; in other cases the form is filled out together at the first-in-person meeting. The majority of these meetings take place in a library meeting room. For a few cases, home visits are done with a colleague.

A staff laptop with the Music & Memory iTunes library is available to bring to these meetings. Music can be played to help develop the list. A presurvey is conducted to gather basic demographic information, for grant reporting purposes, of both the person with dementia and their caregiver.

8. After the meeting, a playlist(s) of songs is created using the survey and the discussion with the person or caretaker. Songs are purchased from iTunes using gift cards, or we work with the patron's own music collection or donated CDs to create the playlist.

9. The playlist is loaded onto an iPod that is loaned to the family. The family can keep the iPod as long as it is useful to them. There is no "due date" for them as with other library materials. The iPod is tracked by the library and can be reprogramed and made available to another family when returned.

10. When the iPod is ready, we schedule another meeting to go over how to use the iPod, and it is given to the family or individual. A follow-up phone call or email is made a couple of weeks afterward to make sure everything is working properly and to answer any questions.

11. After a month or two participants and caretakers are asked to fill out a post-survey to help gauge the success of the program. For example, questions such as these are asked: "In the past week, how often did you feel anxious about the future of your care," "How has the Music & Memory program affected you?"

Suggestions/Tips for Interacting with Residents

- Each experience is different because each individual with dementia is so different.
- In the first six months, there were twelve participants. While the number is a bit smaller than hoped, we are working on promoting and sharing the program more in the community, especially with homebound patrons, area senior centers, and area caregiver groups.
- The feedback received from participants and caretakers has been great and has shown a positive outcome.
- Volunteers are used to help burn CDs, download music onto the iPods, and maintain the iTunes library.

THE MUSIC AND MEMORY PROGRAM

Program by Valerie Lewis, Administrator of Outreach Services, Suffolk Cooperative Library System, Bellport, New York

Description

The Suffolk Cooperative Library System (SCLS) is located on Long Island in New York and consists of fifty-six public libraries. Ms. Valerie Lewis is the administrator of outreach services for the library system and provides outreach training, resources, and programs for employees. Seven or eight years ago, the SCLS was approached by Dan Cohen, founder of the Music & Memory program about donating iPods for the program.

The library system wished to take a different direction with the program and sat down with Mr. Cohen to develop a way to use the program as an outreach service for people with dementia and Alzheimer's disease, who are not living in a senior residential facility. Thus, SCLS created a program for public libraries to loan iPods with individualized music playlists to their patrons who were still living at home.

Supplies/Materials Needed

- Computer with iTunes account
- iPods, MP3 players, headsets
- iTunes gift cards

Program Instructions

1. The Music and Memory program at Suffolk is different than the original program created by Dan Cohen, in that it is offered only to people who have dementia or Alzheimer's and are still living at home.
2. There are fifty-six public libraries in the Suffolk Library System. Each of the library's programs is set up by the individual library. The library provides money to SCLS to coordinate the purchase of iPods or MP3 players, headsets, and iTunes cards to purchase the music. SCLS Outreach Services then coordinates the original ordering of the materials and works with the public library to set up their Music and Memory program.
3. The public library provides staff and caregiver training about the Music and Memory program.
4. For an interested patron or caregiver, staff will ask them to fill out a questionnaire to find the appropriate music.
5. Once the questionnaire is completed, the music is loaded onto the iPod/MP3 player and checked out to the patron.
6. Checkout time varies with the library.

Suggestions/Tips for Interacting with Residents

- This program is designed to be used by patrons with Alzheimer's disease or other dementias, who are still living at home with a caregiver.
- Many Suffolk County public libraries also provide programming in the library for caregivers.
- Before starting the program, fully understand the fundamentals of how it works and who it will benefit. Talk to Mr. Cohen, visit the Music & Memory website, and watch the video "Henry" on the main page.

Program Variations/Alternative Programs

- The program is promoted through the public library newsletter and programs.
- SCLS Outreach Services holds meetings with public library staff twice a year to offer the opportunity to discuss strategies to grow and modify the program as needed.

THE TALES AND TRAVEL MEMORIES PROGRAM

**Program by Stacey McKim, Community and Access Services,
Iowa City Public Library, Iowa City, Iowa**

Description

The Iowa City Public Library's Tales and Travel program is based on the Tales and Travel Memories program, originally developed by the Gail Borden Public Library. This program has been used at different facilities over time, and after consulting with the local Alzheimer's Association, it has been modified a little from the original program. For instance, residents do not read information aloud in case the loss of that skill would cause embarrassment. More content, such as inventions from a country or extra library books with pictures, is brought for those times when the group's abilities are varied or where fewer people have dementia.

Supplies/Materials Needed

- Books from the travel/country section of the library
- Folktales from the selected country
- Interesting facts about the country
- Modern travelogue (e.g., Lonely Planet article)
- Library books with large pictures showing the country
- List of inventions from the country
- An inflatable globe

Program Instructions

1. I bring an inflatable globe, which takes a while to pump up before we officially begin. I joke that it's the warm-up act, which seems to get a chuckle.
2. We start by going around the room to see if anyone has visited the country or have any other connection to it (ancestry, relatives/friends who went there, or any other interest in that culture).
3. One or two folktales from the country are read. Then I read a modern travelogue, such as a short Lonely Planet article about visiting the place.
4. Afterward I share about a dozen short, interesting facts about the country. Each fact might contain about two to five sentences.
5. For the last ten minutes, we pass around library books with large pictures showing scenes and landmarks around the country.
6. Each program ends with a list of inventions from the country.

Suggestions/Tips for Interacting with Residents

- I don't know in advance who will attend the program or what their medical history is. Individuals may also vary widely from visit to visit—disengaged one time and quite vocal the next. I simply try to read their reactions each time and stay light on my feet.
- Encourage the residents to share anything that pops in their head. Conversation is the main reason the library is there. Affirming each person's participation goes a long way in getting the group engaged. I ask follow-up questions, point out locations on the globe or maps, and draw connections between attendees with similar experiences.

- Repeating things so everyone can hear helps to establish a good atmosphere.
- It is uncomfortable, but it's important to wait a while after asking a question or finishing a topic, in case someone is building up to make a comment. I try shuffling my papers/books to give participants time to think.
- Props are appreciated. I've brought currency and souvenirs from countries I've visited, passed around an aromatic jar of garam masala when we talked about India, laid out a beach towel with sea shells for countries with beaches, and so on.
- Bringing more content than recommended by the originators has been helpful on the days when people just aren't chatty or don't have much to share about that country. It's also a way to encourage more conversation for some retirement facilities where fewer people have dementia.
- Hearing will be an issue, so try to get residents to sit close from the start, in a circle or around a table. Some facilities provide a microphone, which might be useful but can also impede participation from the crowd.

Program Variations

- Finding the right folktale can be the hardest part. Many are written in an older style of language or are many pages long. Aim for something short enough that no one falls asleep, adapted in modern language that's easy to understand when projecting your voice, and that has a satisfying ending or gives them a chuckle.
- The Tales and Travel memories program—www.talesandtravelmemories.com—has many more suggestions for this program.

CHAPTER 8

TECHNOLOGY CONNECTIONS

INTRODUCTION

The older adult population is a diverse group with a variety of needs and interests. When it comes to technology, research shows there may be struggles especially among the older members of this population. The youngest of this population may adopt technology quicker, research suggests, perhaps because they had to learn to use technology as part of their job. While there are struggles, once older adults learn how to use technology, they view it as a positive experience. The next generations, Gen X and the millennials, have embraced technology almost from birth and find technology much easier to adapt to.

Public libraries are already part of the technology movement as computer classes are offered in the public library on an ongoing basis. What some libraries have found (as is discussed in the "Appy Hour" program) is that many patrons no longer have a desktop computer at home. They may have a laptop, a smartphone, or a tablet that they use for their computer needs. The equipment that is being used in library programs does not look like what older adults are using at home and may lead to more confusion. Many libraries are beginning to experiment with taking these classes out of the library and to facilities where older adults live and gather.

Adam Chang, instruction and research librarian at Central Ridge Library, Florida, begins this chapter with a discussion of creating and presenting technology classes without a dedicated computer lab. He discusses using this model in a variety of in-house and outreach settings within his library system with positive results. Following his discussion is an outline of the "Appy Hour" program created by Delray Beach Public Library using the techniques presented by Mr. Chang. Mr. Chang's technology model is an example of the type of computer program that could easily be taken off-site. There are other examples of technology programs in this chapter including a mobile computer lab and using virtual reality to enhance outreach programs for older adults.

TECHNOLOGY CLASSES WITHOUT A COMPUTER LAB

By Adam Chang, Instruction and Research Librarian, Citrus County Library System—Central Ridge Library, Florida

Introduction

In 2014, I started working as an instruction and research librarian for the Citrus County Library System. The job appealed to me, because I had experience in a previous library position teaching computer classes.

Teaching classes solidified my plans of becoming a librarian and finishing my MLIS. I believe that providing library patrons with assistance navigating the digital world is an essential service for libraries to provide. Digital literacy is vital.

Challenges and Options

My designated branch didn't have a dedicated computer lab for technology instruction, though we received requests for technology training daily. Typically, our response to patrons looking for a technology class was to direct them to one of the two branches in our library system that had a dedicated lab. I realized that while we had the capacity to meet the needs of our residents within our library system, we weren't always meeting their needs in all of our library branches. Even though our libraries are relatively close (the distance between our coastal region branch and our headquarters library is about ten miles), the distance was too big of an obstacle for many of our patrons.

We faced many challenges trying to meet this need and trying to hold classes in the existing computer area. We couldn't take the patron computers out of operation for the duration of the class, and they weren't set up in a way that would work for instruction. We didn't have the funding to create a new computer lab. I came to realize after talking with many librarians from around the state that they too faced similar challenges. For space and financial reasons, building a dedicated computer lab at every library is not practical. It would be wonderful if every library in the country had a dedicated space for computer use and another for computer instruction, but that's not the reality libraries face. Rather than strive for this level of access, it's much more practical to set a goal of being able to offer some type of technology instruction.

I investigated our options. Could we create a new computer lab for the library? Should we try to get a mobile computer lab, with laptops and accessories that could be accessed on a cart? In my research, I found that many new libraries aren't built with traditional computer labs. Many are built with the design concept of flexible space. Flexible spaces are designed to adapt and change with the library's needs and are based on the philosophy that we can't accurately predict the needs of the future library. These spaces are made to be open ended and are not designed for any sole feature. Library leaders are trying to future-proof spaces so that as the needs of the community change, they can reposition their libraries in a way that meets these needs. Libraries aren't quiet book repositories anymore; instead, they are vibrant hubs for community interaction and gathering.

A few months later, I was assigned to cover a position in a library that did have a dedicated computer lab, our Homosassa branch. I taught biweekly computer classes for several months and began to notice the difficulties that our patrons were having with the traditional model. I often sum this up to people as the "My computer doesn't look like this!" problem. Our computers were made to be as simple for patrons to use as possible, but this simplification does not carry over to their personal devices. For example, in the interest of security, many features are locked down, and using a library computer becomes a very different experience than using a personal device. In addition, I realized that more people were asking more questions about mobile devices than desktop computers. Most of the people using the Internet do not have access through a traditional desktop but instead accessed the Internet on smartphones and tablets. I believe this is where our immediate future in technology training lies. After giving my experiences some thought, I was determined to redesign the classes for our system.

New Library Technology Training

Before I pitched my plan to my supervisors, I made sure to have as detailed of a plan as possible. In my previous experience in libraries, I found this was the best approach. My library administration was supportive of the development of a new service area, but I had to answer two important questions. First, "why is this service important?" and, second, "how much will this cost?"

I gathered statistical information about class attendance and feedback that was presented to me from library patrons. I focused on the questions that were currently being asked—what needs did patrons have right now? The great thing about my plan was that it was high impact, low cost; the only cost was my time researching, developing, and teaching the topics.

Working with Administration

From an administrative IT standpoint, the concerns were about network security and bandwidth. For security, there were clear guidelines that patrons wouldn't be allowed to connect any of their devices directly into the library's network. This is a general policy already in place, but it was reinforced specifically for these types of classes. Bandwidth was also a major concern. Library resources are often stretched and bandwidth is no exception.

With advancements in technology and a heavy reliance on the Internet for daily life, it's difficult for libraries to keep pace and provide enough bandwidth for patron demand. If we run a class and all of a sudden have an extra twenty people sign on to our network with their devices, it could significantly slow down Internet speed for both staff and patrons. To ease this concern, initial classes didn't require the use of the Internet for the class to be instructed. While that might seem counterintuitive to learning how to use a device, we found creative ways around this restriction.

Communicating with Staff

I also talked with some staff about the importance of adapting this new model. Some preferred that equipment is standardized and had concerns about how any devices patrons brought in would differ from our traditionally standardized and locked-down technology. However, I emphasized that while this would make the classes more challenging for us, the same exact concern is what would make the classes more valuable to patrons.

Patrons need to grow in confidence using their own devices. We don't often have the time to build up layers of knowledge with patrons, with a class offered one time or in a short series. While I understand the need for a standardized setup, it's incredibly difficult for someone to go from using a very basic machine to a machine at home that has a near-limitless amount of options.

Program Equipment

For best results, you should have at least a projector and one device (specific to the class) to host a program. For example, it is helpful to have an iPhone when you are teaching an iPhone class and an Android phone for an Android class. The program(s) can be hosted without any of this equipment (you can use screenshots and a PowerPoint or other SlideShare program), but I've found that projecting a device on screen helps with patron understanding. Classes are designed not to require a specific location, but in a variety of locations such as in large community rooms or small labs.

The rest of the equipment is provided by the participants. Not only is it the fastest way to provide instruction, because you don't have to find funding through the library budget or go through a grant process, but I found it also resonates more with the patron. Retention seems to improve with this type of set up. Patrons return to more sessions after taking the initial class, and they are also able to go home and use the same device they used during class to practice and develop questions for future classes.

Creating a Technology Class Curriculum

- Talk to patrons and staff and find out what topics your library isn't covering. Get administration on board, and ensure that you have answers for any of their concerns.

- Write quality curriculum, and be prepared to spend time writing new classes and revising the classes after review by other staff and after a test class. Know that revision will be continuous because of software and hardware updates.

- Start at a very basic level. Don't assume that people already know the basics, and question your own assumptions. Starting at the beginning makes more people feel comfortable and at ease rather than insulted. Manage expectations of participants by labeling classes as introductory or basics, and have a clear description of the material you are going to cover. If you're going to talk about the basics of a phone, make sure you include topics like how to answer a phone, send a text message, and take a picture. Even if the majority of the people in the room are comfortable with answering their phone and it's a review for them, there may be someone who really finds value in a short lesson on how to swipe to answer.

- To be highly effective, these classes can't be a "script"—they must be adaptable and based on the audience's needs. Build in time to focus on areas that patrons are more interested in or need additional assistance. For example, in our alternatives to cable TV class, we've discovered the need to talk about Internet speed, because patrons receive mixed messages from Internet providers about the speed required.

The New Class Model Feedback

Feedback for our new class model has been very positive. From an instruction and research team standpoint, it's allowed the team increased flexibility and creativity in the types of technology instruction we provide. A shift in attitude from "this is what we offer" to "let's try this idea" is evidenced by the over fifty classes we now have rotating throughout all of libraries. Every month the team is bouncing new class ideas around or writing new classes, or a new class is being presented for the first time. It's an exciting process to be part of and is largely due to expanding the ways we provide technology instruction. Once we decided we could provide quality programming outside of our computer labs, the productivity of the team increased.

From a quantitative standpoint, class attendance has increased over the past three years, on average by 20 percent a year. Not only has the interest in mobile classes increased, but these classes have also boosted the attendance numbers of our traditional technology programs. In the past, some patrons have felt that technology programming is too advanced for them. Taking our introductory courses and becoming more comfortable with technology has encouraged them to continue and learn new things.

Patrons and staff are also very vocal about how much they enjoy the new classes. They find them more relatable, more informative, and practical. Patrons are no longer shy about giving staff requests for new class topics. When patrons suggest something or if we find a better way to explain or enhance a class, we work on updating and developing new courses. It's giving staff more freedom to be creative with additional technology programming.

Final Thoughts for Library Staff

Scheduling classes can be difficult, and you may need to experiment with course offerings and day/time of your classes. Consider a balance of several factors: staff availability, network needs, and patron demographics (many seniors prefer early morning, while working professionals prefer evening hours). What's worked for our county is starting each series with iPhone basics and Android basics and then combining the iPhone and Android for more advanced classes, such as "Understanding Apps." We mix these classes with traditional classes. Again, this is not a one-size-fits-all model: you must find out what will work for you with your library's unique characteristics.

In addition, consider grouping classes together under themes. In the past, we've done a series for hurricane/severe weather preparedness (digitally preparing for a disaster) and winter holidays (staying safe online shopping, holiday apps, etc.). Find out what's trending in your community and capitalize on it.

TECHNOLOGY OUTREACH

Technology programming that focuses on mobile devices is constantly evolving. As services become widely adopted and new ones are created, the interest and need continue to grow. Over the past three years, close to fifty technology classes were created by library staff that don't require any specialized technology equipment to be purchased by the library. Every quarter we continue to expand on our classes with new topics. Our topics come from both staff and patron interests. We continue to look for new venues and community partners.

Taking technology programming outside of the library and into the community provides unique challenges. With in-house programming, there's plenty of time to set up a program, test, and troubleshoot. In contrast, outreach programs are difficult in that most won't afford you the luxury of time. Being adaptable and keeping calm under pressure is key. If something isn't working the way it's supposed to, having a backup plan will serve you well, especially in front of an audience in an unfamiliar venue. There are a few things that can be done ahead of your outreach to help identify and minimize potential pitfalls.

Checklist

As you develop your outreach services, it is helpful to create a checklist of materials, location information, and promotional materials. It not only is helpful for the librarian conducting the outreach but also makes expansion of outreach much more efficient.

Tour the Location

Taking a tour of the location where you'll be providing outreach is an excellent first step if given the opportunity. A quick tour can alleviate many concerns and challenges. Identify approximate class size based on the space you'll be presenting, and determine the best method of delivery for your program. In addition, you may want to take note of the equipment available (and test it) so that you can identify the equipment you may want to bring with you. It's always important to test Internet access (if required) so that you are aware of limitations and can alter your presentation ahead of time.

If you don't have the opportunity to take a tour before the day of your outreach, ask to arrive early so that you can get everything set up and test your equipment well before an audience arrives. It gives you time to calmly work out any problems you may encounter, and it provides a more professional appearance.

Regular Communication

Regular communication is very important with outreach services. Establishing a point of contact will help your outreach run smoother and hopefully establish a partnership for future programming.

Call the location ahead of time to remind them that you are going to be visiting their location to provide a technology class. This provides an opportunity to ask questions about the types of information participants are interested in learning about.

Bring handouts with you of the material that will be covered and bring extra. If you run out of handouts at an outreach, you don't have the luxury of printing more from your printer. Be sure to bring additional promotional materials with you that talk about other library services. If residents can't make it physically to the library, perhaps they can still get a library card and take advantage of e-book services.

Future Outreach

Speak with your point of contact and see if there are other partnerships within the library that they might be interested in. Maybe they'd like another staff member to come in and lead a craft, or perhaps they would like a deposit collection to help their residents have access to more materials.

EXAMPLES OF TECHNOLOGY PROGRAMS

Apple iPhone: Getting Started

In this class we will learn the basics of Apple's iPhone. We'll cover some of the most commonly used features of smartphones, including, apps, settings, using the camera, connecting to the Internet, and sending text messages.

Android Phones: Getting Started

Introduction to the Android phone: learn how to send and receive text messages, take and send pictures, navigate different apps, connect to the Internet, and more.

Understanding Apps

Find out what an app is, how it works, and where you can find one. Learn how to purchase and install apps onto your device and how to manage them once they're there. You will also be provided with a list of popular apps to get you started.

Alternatives to Cable TV

Join us for an informative presentation that will introduce and discuss various alternatives to cable TV. Learn about streaming, the different devices available for streaming media, and some of the most popular apps available. We'll discuss the benefits and drawbacks of these alternatives and ways to help you get started.

Getting Smart with Smart Homes

What exactly makes a smart home so smart? Join us as we discuss what a smart home is and what kind of technology is involved in smart devices and the Internet of Things. This presentation will discuss the basics of smart technology and discuss popular devices such as the Amazon Alexa, Nest Thermostat, and the Philips Hue Smart Hub.

APPLE IPHONE: GETTING STARTED

**Program by Adam Chang, Instruction and Research Librarian
Citrus County Library System—Central Ridge Library, Florida**

Description

This is one of the technology programs created at the Citrus County Library System. It was both used in-house and taken to other sites, including senior care centers. It is suggested that the participants have some familiarity with smartphones, have an email address, and know their Apple ID and password. During this program, participants learned how to use the different buttons on their smartphones, send and receive messages, take and send pictures, navigate different apps, and connect to the Internet. A handout with pictures and text was created and handed out to participants.

Supplies/Materials Needed

- iPhone
- Email address, Apple ID, and password
- Connection to a projector and monitor
- Handout

Program Instructions

1. **Buttons**
   - While all types of smartphones are different, most have a standard set of buttons.
   - Point out the common buttons on iPhones (ringer switch, volume and sleep buttons, app icon, home screen pages, home button, and so on).
   - The first thing you're going to want to do on any device nowadays is connect to the Wi-Fi service.

2. **Connecting to Wi-Fi**
   - Locate and tap on the Settings icon.
   - Tap on Wi-Fi icon.
   - Check that your Wi-Fi is turned on (i.e., that the switch icon next to Wi-Fi is green).
     *Note about the green switch feature: Consider this an on/off switch. When it is green, that means it's on. When it's white/grayed out, that means it's off.
     You tap on it to switch between on and off.
   - Under Choose a Network, tap on the network you want to connect to.
   - The network you've selected should show up under Wi-Fi with a blue checkmark next to it.

3. **Adding a contact**
   - Adding contacts to your phonebook eliminates the need to memorize phone numbers. Your contact information can contain as little information as a name and phone number. More advanced features like adding a photo, email address, and home address are possible as well.
   - To add a contact:
     - Tap on the Contacts icon.
     - At the top-right corner of your screen, tap on the "+" icon.

○ A menu will appear with fillable options where you may enter as much or as little information as you'd like. For example:

  ▫ Tap on Company and type: Homosassa Public Library.

  ▫ Tap the "+" next to add phone—type in the library's phone number: 352–628–5626

  ▫ Tap the "+" next to add URL—type in the library's website address: www.citruslibraries.org

  ▫ Tap the "+" next to add address—type in the library's address:

    4100 S Grandmarch Avenue

    Homosassa, FL 34446

  ▫ In the top-right corner of your screen, tap Done.

4. **Dialing a number**

  • If you want to call someone but don't have them stored in your contacts, you can dial their number manually using Phone.

    ○ Press the Home button to go back to home if you haven't already.

    ○ Tap on the Phone icon.

    ○ Notice that there are five tabs at the bottom of the screen. By tapping on any one of these, you can go to your Favorites, Recents, Contacts, Keypad, or Voicemail.

    ○ Tap on Keypad if you are not there already.

    ○ Type in the number you would like to dial.

    ○ Press the green button to dial the number.

    ○ Once you hit dial, options such as mute, keypad, speaker, and contacts will be made available to you.

  • Facetime and add call will also appear if the option is available.

5. **Sending a message**

  • Smartphones make it easy to send text and picture messages.

  • Tap on the Messages icon.

  • Here is where all your current conversations (people you are messaging) will be listed.

  • Tap on the New Message symbol at the top right.

  • Tap on the "+" symbol at the top right to add a contact.

  • Once their name appears, tap in the text box to begin typing your message.

  • Once you've finished typing, tap on the blue up arrow to Send the message.

  • In order to go back to your list of conversations, tap on (back arrow) at the top-left corner of the screen.

6. **Sending a picture message**

  • You can also send pictures through messaging.

  • Tap on the Messages icon if you haven't already.

  • From here, you can either select a conversation you currently have listed or begin a new one. Note that if you start a new one, you will have to enter a contact before you can send a picture.

  • Tap on the Camera icon.

  • You can either select a photo from those listed on your phone or take a new one.

  • If you want to include text, do so now.

- Once your message is complete, tap Send.
- Note that picture messages are much bigger than simple text messages and as such may take longer to go through than your standard message. If you have slower Internet or poor reception when you send it, the message may not go through. If that happens, check your signal and try to resend.

7. Apps

- Smartphones utilize apps. "App" is a shorthand way to say "software application." If you are familiar with using a computer, apps are very similar to the programs you use there. Your phone comes pre-loaded with a variety of basic apps, and you can download more from your app store.
- Some app suggestions to get you started: Google Maps, Skype, Yelp, Pandora, Goodreads, Pinterest, Dropbox, Words with Friends.

8. **Clock app**

- The clock on your phone is a great app to learn how to use, because it's simple and can be very helpful if you ever need an alarm clock or stopwatch. To set an alarm:
    ◦ Tap on the Clock icon to open the app.
    ◦ You'll notice at the bottom of the screen a list of tabs, just like in your phone app. There's World Clock, Alarm, Bedtime, Stopwatch, and Timer.
    ◦ Tap on Alarm.
    ◦ Tap on the "+" to add a new alarm.
    ◦ Select a time.
    ◦ You have various other options to choose from, such as if you want the alarm to repeat, if you want to give it a label, if you want to change the sound of the alarm, and if you want snooze to be on.
    ◦ Once you have gone through all that, tap Save at the top-right corner of the screen.

9. **Camera app**

- Every smartphone has at least one camera built in. The camera can be used to take pictures, record videos, chat, or run in tandem with many different apps. The basics of using the camera include knowing how to turn the camera on, how to take pictures, and how to retrieve pictures you have taken.
- When using your smartphone, you will find several different ways to access your camera. The most common way is by pressing the Home button and tapping on the Camera icon.
- Once you open your camera app, you'll notice your screen displays everything the camera is pointed at. Tapping on the screen will bring your shot into focus.
- If you are trying to take a selfie, tap on the icon that will switch your camera around to face you.
- Once you have everything the way you want, tap on the white circle to take the shot.

10. **Pictures**

- If your camera app is open, you can access your pictures by tapping on the thumbnail picture at the bottom left corner of the screen. Or you can press the Home button and then tap on the Photos icon.
- From here you can look at your camera roll, create an album, edit and share photos, and a lot more.

11. **Closing apps**

- It's a good habit to close apps once you are finished with them. Just pressing the home button to take you back will not close the app. Every app you open will still continue to run in the "background" until you officially close it out.

- To close your apps:
  - Press the Home button once to take you back if you are not already there.
  - Press the Home button twice in quick succession.
  - All of the apps you currently have open will arrange themselves horizontally for you to thumb through.
  - For each app you want to close, simply swipe upwards.
  - Continue until you have closed all your apps.

12. **Removing apps**

- You may find you have too many apps, or you don't use a particular app anymore, or you just don't like an app you've installed. In any case, don't worry! You can remove and rearrange any apps you want, however you want.
- Tap and hold the app you want to (re)move.
- After a second, all of your apps will start to wiggle in their places with an "X" appearing at the top-left corner of each.
- Tap on the "X" of each app you want to remove.
- Confirm your selection.
- Once you're finished, press the Home button.
- All your apps should stop wiggling and the "X"s should disappear.

  * Note that a few select apps that come with your iPhone or iPad cannot be removed from your device.

13. **Safari**

- Safari is the web browser (same as Internet Explorer, Firefox, Google Chrome, etc.) that comes preinstalled on every iPhone, iPad, and Apple computer. From here you can browse the Internet, bookmark links, and share websites.
- You can have multiple tab windows in Safari open at the same time. And just like with your apps, it's a good habit to go through and make sure that you are closing out all those tabs once you are done using them.
- To close your Safari window tabs one at a time:
  - Tap near the bottom of the screen to bring up your Safari options.
  - Tap on the Tabs icon.
  - Your currently open tabs will line up vertically for you to thumb through.
  - To close a window, tap on the small "X" at the top-left corner.
  - To close your Safari windows all at once:
    - Tap and hold on the Tabs icon.
    - You will be prompted to close all tabs.

  * Note that you will always have one window remaining.

14. **Notifications**

- Whenever you get a new email, message, tweet, Facebook post, or phone update, a red circle with a number will appear at the top-right corner of the app in question, letting you know there's something new there for you.
- It's always a smart idea to keep on top of these, especially if it's an update under your Settings.

15. **Security**

   - Now that you have a smartphone, it is recommended that you take a few steps to protect both your phone and any information stored inside it.

16. **Selecting a case**

   - Most smartphones do not come with a case, but to help reduce the risk of damage to your phone, it's recommended that you keep it in a case.
   - Cases can vary in style and price. They are also rated for a variety of risks. The most common risk associated with smartphones comes from dropping them from a height of about three to four feet.
   - Be sure to read the package of the case you plan to buy to see what types of damage it will protect from.
   - Most will protect from small drops as well as minimize dust and debris.

17. **Locking your smartphone**

   - Taking a few minutes and setting a password for your smartphone should give you peace of mind and prevent most people from accessing your information without your permission.
   - A password for smartphones can be one or more of the following:
      - A four-digit PIN
      - A pattern you designate
      - Your fingerprint

   - To set a password:
      - Tap on the Settings icon.
      - Under Settings, tap on Touch ID & Passcode.
      - Select the type of passcode you want.
      - Type in your passcode and tap Done.

   * Be sure to remember this code!

18. **Data**

   - Cell phones use data to access the Internet. It's important to find out from your phone provider what type of data plan you have. Many plans are now unlimited, but some do exist with monthly limits. If you exceed your monthly limit, your phone provider will charge you a fee.
   - Turning off your phone:
      - Pressing the power button to put your iPhone to sleep and again to wake it up is not the same as powering your iPhone off and on. When your phone is "sleeping," it's still on, which is why you still get phone calls and message dings and why your battery continues to deplete even when you're not on it.
   - To turn your phone off completely:
      - Press and hold the power button until the screen changes and prompts you to "slide to power off."
      - Drag your finger left to right across the slider bar to power off.
   - You should make it a habit to power off your iPhone at least once a week. It doesn't even need to be for more than a few minutes at a time. This way your phone can better "tidy up" after itself and finish installing any updates that require restarts in order to be finalized.

APPY HOUR

**Program by Loanis Menendez, Head of Reference, and
Alyson Walzer, Reference Assistant
Delray Beach Public Library, Delray Beach, Florida**

Description

This program came about after attending Adam Chang's program titled "Technology Classes without the Computer Lab: How to Rethink Technology Offerings and Expand Outreach Opportunities @ Your Library" at the Florida Library Association meeting in 2017. The Delray Beach Public Library has a large fifty-five-plus population that attends programs and classes. Computer classes have typically included the basics—Word, Excel, Gmail, and so on—but in the last year or so, people were asking for help with their phones or tablets and no longer owned a desktop or laptop computer. Seniors were asking about eBay and Craigslist, Offer Up, Let Go, and how to use apps.

To meet this need, classes were broken down into the basics—what the apps are for, how to use them, and then give a demonstration on how they work. Follow-up and a one-on-one appointment were also set up to go over the information again. The classes most often asked for were shopping online, streaming videos and music, banking online, GPS, editing photos and videos, and password managers. The other apps chosen were based on what the staff thought were important. This program was originally presented in the library, though with a few modifications the staff hopes to take it off-site.

Supplies/Materials Needed

- A seventy-five-inch Touch Screen Smart Board was used. Devices were connected to it so the apps could be demonstrated. The Smart Board has a browser and inputs to allow other things to be displayed, such as a computer or anything else that has an HDMI (high-definition multimedia interface) connection or adaptor.
- Slide show for each class depending on the topic: The classes included e-books, e-magazines and digital audio, editing and managing photos and video, streaming music and videos, GPS apps including Waze and Maps and Google Maps, Amazon Shopping, how to stop RoboCalls, iWatch, iPhone and Siri, social media: Facebook, Instagram, and Twitter.
- Hotspot dedicated to the class.

Program Instructions

1. A one-hour "Appy Hour" was offered each month from June to August.
2. For each program one librarian acted as the lead instructor, while the other librarians were on hand to help out in the classroom. Classes were open to staff members too, especially those about RbDigital, Gateway, Hoopla, and Overdrive.
3. All android users were separated from the IOS users. While the presenter taught the class, the other librarians stayed with each group to help with download, catch-up, and so on.
4. Each class focused on certain apps or topics. Lessons were very informal, and we demonstrated the apps that we use the most but made a list of comparable apps so they could "shop around."
5. A hotspot dedicated to the class was used so there were no interruptions in connectivity or with the Wi-Fi being slow.

6. The following program is for the Editing and Managing Photos and Videos class. The aim of this class was to show how to make the best of the photography features on a phone or tablet. The lead teacher used Google Slides for each point and then showed the participants how to use it on their device. The slide show followed the following steps.

   a. **Shoot some pictures or video.** The lead teacher talked about different phones and the common features of each. Features included focus, high dynamic range, first shooting, live photo (on IOS), and Motion Photo (new on Samsung and Google). General tips and tricks, orientation, and what else your phone can do such as other popular apps were also included.

   b. **Review and select the ones you want to keep**. Edit the selected photos (image editing basics). If you'd like to explore features that go beyond the basic photo editing on your phone's native photos app, try one of these apps: Snapseed, Pixlr.

   c. **Edit the selected photos.**

   d. **Share your favorites.** You can share photos and videos from the Photos and Gallery apps or from Facebook, Instagram, messaging, email, and other services. Social media apps also allow you to shoot photos from their apps. You can decide which way works best for your workflow.

   e. **Organize your photos and videos.** The Photos and Gallery apps automatically organize your photos into albums based on category (videos, live photos, panoramas, etc.) or the app used to create or edit the photo. You can't delete these default albums, but you can create your own albums.

   f. **Archiving and backing up your photos.** Apple and Google provide seamless ways to synchronize your photos from your iPhone or Android phone to their cloud services. Syncing makes your whole photo collection available in the photo apps on any device logged into your Apple iCloud or Google Photos account. Apple provides 5 GB of free storage; Google provides 15 GB for free. You can pay for more storage if you need it. Or you can upload your photo and video collection to your laptop or desktop computer by connecting your phone to your computer with a USB cable, or transfer them wirelessly with Bluetooth or Wi-Fi.

7. You won't need all of these steps for every photo and video you shoot. You can choose from among the tips we'll share to create the workflow that works best for you.

8. More resources:

   • iPhone Photography School

   • GCFLearnFree.org online tutorials:

     ◦ Image editing 101

     ◦ Instagram

9. Books about online photo sharing: Books about specific mobile devices can be found in the Delray Beach Public Library's nonfiction collection at this call number: 004.167.

10. From Apple Support: Organize and find your photos; take and edit photos with your iPhone, iPad, and iPod touch iCloud Photo Library, the photos app on your Mac.

11. From Google Support: Google photos help Google Photos on Android devices.

Suggestions/Tips for Interacting with Residents

• While this was originally presented as an in-house library program, modifications can be made so it can be done at other facilities. Modifications would depend on what the facility would be able to help with, such as a large TV or monitor and a large-enough space. A newer TV would allow the hookups needed as long as you have an HDMI cable and use the input to display on the screen.

- A laptop and video projector with screen (or white wall) would work too for display. There would not be touch screen interactivity, but if you have a wireless mouse/remote, that would help advance presentations.

Program Variations

- Using volunteers would be great, as long as they are comfortable with the material and knowledgeable.

VIRTUAL REALITY AND AUGMENTED REALITY

Introduction

The technology of virtual reality (VR) and augmented reality (AR) once found in books, 3D movies, early-flight stimulators, and stereoscopes is becoming a reality for consumers, thanks to advances in technology. VR immerses the user into a completely simulated environment, while AR provides additional information through apps, headsets, or QR codes to supplement real surroundings. Both VR and AR reached consumers first through gaming and entertainment and have become more available as informational and educational programs for older adults (Dudley, 2018; Pope, 2018). The lower costs of devices and the extensive collection of available programs are a valuable resource for libraries that provide lifelong learning programs for older adults. VR and AR have been beneficial in combating isolation in older adults and provide an opportunity to travel to places they are no longer able to travel to through Google Expedients or to visit their childhood neighborhoods. It has also been shown to be beneficial for persons with dementia to help them feel more connected to their life (Pope, 2018).

VR devices have improved over the past several decades. Some libraries are beginning to offer a VR and AR program using headsets such as the HTC Vive or the Oculus Rift. These headsets are at the higher end of the price range. They are comfortable and fit over prescription eyeglasses and some have additional features for those who are far sighted or near sighted. At the lower end of the price range, there is the Google Cardboard headset that uses a smartphone. VR has some positive attributes, especially for older adults who may be socially isolated. Virtual travel allows an individual to travel digitally when they can no longer physically travel. VR technology is also making it possible to share real experiences digitally with family and friends (Dudley, 2018).

Carroll County Public Library Virtual Reality Program

The Carroll County Public Library in New Windsor, Maryland, has developed a VR program using a variety of VR and AR technologies for its patrons. Carroll County Public Library has used VR with all ages and found that older adults were as eager to try out new technology as much as any other age groups. Using Chicago Style Manual, edition 17 please add J. Bishop and D. Stoltz (personal e-mail communication, September 2018) provided multiple examples of how AR and VR are being used at the the Carroll County Public Library. VR can be used as a virtual field trip to enhance any type of program, especially as more content becomes available.

The availability of VR during a program provides access to a new technology that most still don't have access to and haven't yet experienced. For example, the Google Expedition VR kits (phone-based VR viewer) were used to enhance an adult book club program to virtually visit Appalachia when discussing John Grisham's *Gray Mountain.* Open houses provide an opportunity for the public to try different VR demo experiences.

Virtual Reality Equipment

There are a variety of VR and AR technologies available. The following are some of the devices Carroll County Public Library has used for programs.

Phone Based—Google Cardboard. A fairly inexpensive program can be done with a smartphone and Google Cardboard goggles that are manufactured by several different companies. The most expensive device is the smartphone if customers do not have a phone.

Google Expeditions. This is an immersive app that allows the user to explore the world through VR and AR. These kits are powered by the Best Buy Education program and include teacher and student devices and viewers, a router, and chargers. The kits can also be self-assembled with phones, card-board goggles, and a tablet. Higher-priced devices such as Oculus Rifts and HTC Vives that require an expensive computer to run them can also be used.

The Google Expedition program consists of thousands of expeditions which are downloaded. Each expedition consists of five to twenty, 360-degree photographs of a single topic. There are apps that let you physically walk through famous paintings or that take you to outer space in a space rocket. Other expeditions include the Great Wall of China, Buckingham Palace, and the White House.

To present the program the instructor holds the tablet and controls what participants see. Participants hold the cardboard viewers and are immersed in each image. They can look in all directions, even spin around, and look at all the details. Facts about each image may be displayed for them on a tablet, which they can then read aloud.

PC Based—HTC Vive and Oculus Rift + Touch. The high-end VR experiences (Vive and Oculus) are a one-user-at-a-time experience, so other activities are a must. Often two Google Expedition kits (twenty phone-based viewers) are available to offer more simultaneous use for a program offering/enhancement.

High-end, PC-based VR with the HTC Vive and Oculus Rift provides more interactive and immersive experiences with high-level optics. The HTC Vive and Oculus Rift + Touch both require VR-ready PCs (which have a higher-level graphics card than a typical computer).

REFERENCES

Dudley, David. December 2018/January 2019. "Oh, The Places You'll Go: Soon You'll Travel the World, Visit Grandkids and See Your Doctor without Leaving Your Living Room Thanks to Virtual Reality." *AARP The Magazine*.

Pope, Hannah. August/September 2018. "Virtual and Augmented Reality in Libraries." *Library Technology Reports* 54 (no. 6). pp. 5–25. https://search.proquest.com/openview/1b197fb6b301c1c61e67078dbc41d0c4/1?pq-origsite=gscholar&cbl=37743.

OLD AND NEW TECH: VIRTUAL REALITY AND STEREOSCOPIC DEVICES

Program by Jennifer Bishop, Online Services and Emerging Technologies Supervisor, and Dorothy Stoltz, Director of Community Engagement Carroll County Public Library, New Windsor, Maryland

Description

Carroll County Public Library is fortunate to have senior volunteers who read widely, are comfortable with computers, and love history. They are a natural choice to present programs for local senior centers. A superb senior volunteer by the name of Hash was taught by his father how to "see" in 3D without the use of a device, by training the eyes to adjust and focus in a specific way. As a result he became interested in the history of two- and three-dimensional technologies as a hobby, researching extensively and collecting stereoscopic devices (devices that were used to give the illusion of depth from two-dimensional images) from the 1800s and 1900s. Therefore, it only made sense that Hash would be involved in a virtual reality program at the senior centers.

Hash provided a slide show presentation on the history of stereoscopic devices along with an interactive demonstration of the devices. Participants then had a hands-on opportunity to experience virtual reality using the Vive. Other augmented reality (AR) items such as take-home temporary tattoos and coloring sheets also featured were popular to share with grandchildren.

Supplies/Materials Needed

- A space in the back of the room for the VR Vive, ideally twelve by twelve feet, but eight by eight feet can work.
- Wi-Fi capability (a phone has been used as a hotspot too).
- Electrical outlet.
- Two tables set up in front for the vintage stereoscopic devices as activity stations.
- Vintage stereoscopic devices, such as 1800s' stereoscope stereo viewer and stereo cards for viewing nature, pocket stereoscope used by the military in World War II to examine stereoscopic pairs of aerial photographs, 1900s' view-masters and reels of tourist sites, and today's Google Expeditions.
- Sound system, if possible.
- PowerPoint capability for interesting visuals.

Program Instructions

1. Set up the Vive and the hands-on stations. Allow at least sixty to ninety minutes to set everything up.
2. Library staff introduces the program and briefly talks about how the library is changing—including highlighting 3D printing and laser engraving services and demonstrating the AR temporary tattoos, coloring sheets, and AR interactives.
3. Volunteers or librarians present "old tech" information using PowerPoint but interweave and build up excitement about the upcoming hands-on opportunity with the Vive.
4. The librarian or other staff facilitates using the Vive and allows everyone who wants to take a turn. Participants either stand or sit in a chair, whichever works best for them. While people are in the queue, our volunteers offer hands-on activities using vintage stereoscopic devices as well as the Google Expeditions.

5. In addition, everyone has the opportunity to see AR up close through iPad demonstrations and can take home AR activity cards, coloring sheets, and temporary tattoos.

6. AR images are demonstrated through temporary tattoos, coasters, activity/rack cards produced by the company Balti Virtual. For temporary tattoos visit the HoloTats website, http://www.holotats.com, where you can purchase temporary tattoos. Download the HoloTats app (produced by Balti Virtual) for free on a smartphone or an iPad, and then apply it to the image on the card. There may be a small fee for the temporary tattoos. For an idea of how it works, check out this YouTube demonstration: https://www .youtube.com/watch?v=wjyI3v7hZf0.

7. The coloring sheets work in a similar way. Go to Quivervision, http://www.quivervision.com, and print out the coloring sheets. Download the Quivervision app, color the sheet, and apply the app to the image on the sheet. There may be a small fee for the app and coloring sheets. For an idea of how it works, check out this YouTube demonstration: https://youtu.be/tBYm53L79YY.

Suggestions/Tips for Interacting with Residents

- A benefit for the library offering senior programs away from the library, especially to its retirement community settings, is that seniors learn more about and strengthen their connection to the library. This gives seniors an opportunity for meaningful ways to contribute their time, insights, and talents as volunteers and/or financially to something that interests and inspires them.

  For example, a library builds relationships with individuals who may end up presenting library programs and/or donating to a special library fundraising campaign or leaving a legacy gift in their will.

- It's always good to explain the technology a little first and explain everything that's going to happen before letting people put on a headset. With the cardboards it's less crucial, because it's easy to just move your arm away if you don't enjoy the sensation. It's important to remind everyone not to touch or bump each other while they're immersed in VR.

Program Variations

- The high-end VR experiences (Vive and Oculus) are one-user-at-a-time experiences, so other activities are a must. Google Expedition kits (twenty phone-based viewers) are available to offer more simultaneous use for a program offering/enhancement.

- Build a traveling exhibit of artifacts using local history and AR to accompany a program.

- Volunteers also presented programs about the Union Mills Homestead, an important early industrial complex—gristmill and tannery—in Carroll County's history with national significance as the family homestead of Sargent Shriver, the first director of the Peace Corps.

WEB ON WHEELS BUS: MOBILE COMPUTER LAB

Missoula Public Library, Missoula, Montana

Description

The Web on Wheels (WOW) bus began in 2011 after the Missoula Public Library received a Broadband Technology Opportunities Program grant. The focus of the grant was to bring Internet connectivity to rural areas outside of Missoula. Initially, the bus traveled eighty miles (one way) to communities the library identified that might benefit from the service. A stipulation of the grant was that the bus would not carry library materials (books, CDs, or DVDs). It was to be a mobile computer lab.

Supplies/Materials Needed

- Book mobile or bus.
- The bus is equipped with eight laptop stations for participants and two stations for staff.
- Initially, the mobile bus did not carry any library materials. After the initial grant period ended, a small collection of library books and audio visual materials were added.
- Participant's electronic device.

Program Instructions

1. After the initial grant period, additional scheduled bus stops were expanded to include locations within city limits.
2. These include weekly visits to senior living facilities. In addition to these facilities, the bus visits schools, a homeless shelter, and public housing weekly.
3. Questions regarding phones, tablets, and e-readers are popular.
4. We encourage patrons to arrive with their devices, and we'll spend an entire stop (three hours) working on issues with them, if necessary.

Suggestion/Tip for Interacting with Residents

- Encourage patrons to arrive with their devices.

CONCLUSION

If you are reading this, you have reached the end of the book. Whether you read this book from cover to cover or jumped around to different sections, it is my hope that you have come away with an appreciation and greater understanding of who the older adult population is and how libraries can become more involved in providing services and programs for them. The older adult population is growing and will continue to grow over the next several decades. This population is made up of different generations with diverse backgrounds, interests, and needs. Many are not able to visit the library, and unlike previous generations, they can be found living in and visiting a variety of locations. They may be living at home, in residential or assisted living facilities, or with family members, attending adult day care and memory cafés. Libraries have a role to play in extending their programs and services beyond the library walls and into the community.

I encourage you to look at what your community and library are doing for this population and ask if there is more that can be done. Present information to administration and staff as to the importance of understanding the needs of the older adult population, and encourage them to become more involved in providing programs and services. Try some of the programs in this book in your own outreach presentations, or modify them to meet your needs. Reach out to the libraries that were willing to include their program outline in this book, and talk to them about their programs. Identify other organizations in your community that are working with older adults and partner with them. Share your programs and ideas for older adults with one another. Talk about programming for older adults at adult services meetings, at state and national professional meetings, in the literature, and on social media.

The inability to find information about programming in the literature and on social media was the impetus that started this project. As I come to the end of this book, I am encouraged by the way some libraries have stepped outside of the traditional programming box and are looking for new/additional ways to serve older adults who are not able to visit the library. My hope is that more libraries will also take that step and be willing to make changes to meet the needs of their older adult population. I also hope that in the future we will see more discussion about programming for this special population in professional meetings, in the literature, and on social media.

RESOURCE DIRECTORY

GENERAL INFORMATION ABOUT OLDER ADULTS

Administration on Aging (AoA). https://acl.gov/about-acl/administration-aging (promotes quality care of older adults with services and programs for living independently, nutrition and health).

American Association of Retired Persons. www.aarp.org (resources, statistics, research).

American Library Association: Older Adults. www.ala.org/tools/atoz/older-adults.

American Library Association: Reference and User Services Association (RUSA). 2017. "Guidelines for Library Services with 60+ Audience, Best Practices." http://www.ala.org/rusa/sites/ala.org.rusa/files/content/resources/guidelines/60plusGuidelines2017.pdf (guidelines for providing library programming to older adults).

Grants. https://www.grants.gov.

Programming Librarian. http://programminglibrarian.org (a website of the American Library Association Public Programs Office with resources and connections for libraries to share programming ideas).

DEMOGRAPHICS

American Association of Retired Persons. www.aarp.org (resources, statistics, research).

American Community Survey (ACS). https://www.census.gov/programs-surveys/acs/ (housing and population changes within the community).

American FactFinder—Census Bureau. https://factfinder.census.gov/faces/nav/jsf/pages/index.xhtml (community data).

National Institute on Aging. https://nia.nih.gov (research on health and aging).

ADULT STORY TIMES AND LITERACY

Assistive Technology and Tips for Persons with Blindness and Low Vision. https://www.asgcladirect.org/resources/blindness-and-low-vision/ (information about interacting with persons with loss of vision, hearing, and cognitive and physical disabilities).

ElderSong Publications. https://www.eldersong.com (activity newsletters and publications).

Fifties Website. https://fiftiesweb.com/ (cars, fashion, music pop culture/history from the 1950s and 1960s).

Library of Congress. https://www.loc.gov (variety resources including Baseball Americana exhibit and other baseball highlights, digital photo collection, historical programs and resources).

Library of Congress Center for the Book. www.read.gov/cfb/ (promotes reading and literature, links to resources for book lovers and librarians by subject, poems, author webcasts, digital collections, and booklists).

Stores and Websites That Sell Items/Props from Past Decades That Could Be Used with Programs: Cracker Barrel Store, www.crackerbarrel.com; Betty's Attic, www.bettysattic.com; Vermont Country Store, www.vermontcoun trystore.com.

ART- AND LITERATURE-BASED PROGRAMMING

Bell, Virginia, and David Troxel. 2007. *Best Friends Book of Alzheimer's Activities*, two volumes. Baltimore: Health Professions Press, Inc.
Heinly, La Doris. 2010. *Memories in the Making*. La Doris (resource for tips and philosophy).

MEMORY AND MIND PROGRAMMING

"Alive Inside: A Story of Music and Memory." http://www.aliveinside.us/#land (documentary about the work of Dan Cohen and his experiences in using music to elicit memories in nursing home residents diagnosed with dementia).
Alzheimer's and Memory Cafés. http://www.alzheimerscafe.com/public.html.alzheimerscafe.com/Welcome.html (information about creating monthly cafés for individuals with memory loss along with their caregivers; the concept of the café is to provide an atmosphere that is supportive and engaging and fun.)
Alzheimer's Association. https://www.alz.org (information and statistics on Alzheimer's disease and dementia).
American Library Association—Alzheimer's and Related Dementias Interest Group (IGARD). https://www.asgcla direct.org/interest-groups/ (general page).
American Library Association—Alzheimer's and Related Dementias Interest Group (IGARD). https://www.asgcla direct.org/resources/alzheimers-related-dementias-interest-group-igard/ (resources by subject).
American Library Association—Alzheimer's and Related Dementias Interest Group (IGARD). https://www.asgcla direct.org/resources/patrons-with-alzheimers-and-related-dementias/ (accessibility toolkit).
Dementia Friendly America. http://www.dfamerica.org (nationwide effort to bring all aspects of a community together to support a dementia-friendly community).
Dementia Friendly America Library Sector Guide. https://static1.squarespace.com/static/559c4229e4b0482682e8d f9b/t/57c89321b3db2b985d790602/1472762658227/DFA-SectorGuide-Library.pdf (outlines ways that libraries can participate in the dementia-friendly efforts going on across the country).
Family Caregiver Alliance: National Center on Caregiving. https://www.caregiver.org/ (information, support, and resources for family caregivers).
International Federation of Library Associations: Guidelines for Library Services to Persons with Dementia by Helle Arendup Mortensen and Gyda Skat Nielsen. 2007. https://archive.ifla.org/VII/s9/nd1/Profrep104.pdf.
Library Memory Project. https://www.librarymemoryproject.org (information about the memory café and library partnerships in Waukesha, Washington, and Milwaukee counties, in Wisconsin).
Memory Cafés and Libraries: The Perfect Fit, Kernel of Knowledge Services. http://programminglibrarian.org/ programs/memory-caf%C3%A9 (archived webinar about creating library memory cafés).
Music & Memory. https://musicandmemory.org/ (information, training, and research about the effects of music on memory).
Programming Librarian—Program Model: Memory Café. 2017. http://programminglibrarian.org/programs/ memory-caf%C3%A9 (memory café program at Shrewsbury, Massachusetts, Public Library).
Public Libraries Online—Memory Care at Your Library. http://publiclibrariesonline.org/2016/09/memory-care-at-your-library/ (discusses the use of memory cafés in libraries around the country).
Tales and Travel Memories. http://talesandtravelmemories.com (travel programs for persons with early dementia and Alzheimer's disease created in conjunction with Gail Borden Library; includes resources and information).
Tales and Travel Memories. http://talesandtravelmemories.com/wp-content/uploads/2019/04/Tales-Travel-Checklist-11-20-18.pdf. (Under the "For Librarians" tab there are tips and suggestions on conducting successful programs. A Facilitation checklist is also available.)
Wisconsin Alzheimer's Institute. "Best Practice Guides." http://www.wai.wisc.edu/publichealth/guides.html (guides about dementia-friendly libraries and memory cafés in Wisconsin).